CON

Walking the Rivelin

A pocket guide to the industrial heritage and natural history of the Rivelin Valley

5th edition

Original research and previous editions by Keith Kendall.

Further research, additions and trail guide by Sue Shaw, with contributions from RVCG Committee members.

Cover, layout design and mini-maps by Holly Ormrod-Stebbings.

Acknowledgments

Thanks go to: Sheffield Archives, Sheffield Library Service, Sheffield Local Studies Library, Museums Sheffield, Sheffield Star Newspapers.

Thanks also to RVCG members, family and friends, who have read various versions, walked the route and made helpful suggestions for the latest update of this book.

The JG Graves Charitable Trust kindly provided financial support towards the publication of this book.

Photographs:

Copyright in the photographs remains with the original photographer or source.
Sheffield Archives and Museums Sheffield kindly gave permission to reproduce images from their collections.
Uncredited recent photographs are by Keith Kendall, Sue Shaw and Joan Buckland (RVCG).
We are very grateful to Alan and Andy Jones for supplying the photographs of birds and butterflies.

First printed 1998 and with revisions in 1998, 2000 and 2005.
5th edition published in 2014 by:
        Arc Publishing and Print
        166 Knowle Lane, Bents Green, Sheffield S11 9SJ
        Tel: 07809 172872. Web: www.sheffieldbooks.co.uk
ISBN: 978-1-906722-36-4

INFORMATION FOR VISITORS

Start: *Rivelin Valley Road* (A6101) at Malin Bridge. Nearest postcode: S6 5FE.
OS grid reference: SK 3258 8930.

End: *Rails Road car park*, close to the junction of Rivelin Valley Road with the A57 Manchester Road. Nearest postcode: S6 5SJ. OS grid reference SK 2912 8725.

Description: A scenic 3 mile (*c*. 5 km) walk upstream along the lower reaches of the Rivelin valley, starting from Malin Bridge and ending at **Rivelin Corn Mill** (Rails Road). At an easy pace the walk should take between 1½ and 3 hours (excluding return), depending on time taken to look for wildlife and the historical remains. The trail is not waymarked, but is easy to find as it follows the river. Return via the same route, or using some of the many other footpaths and lanes in the area; alternatively, return by walking for 20–30 minutes up to Lodge Moor, Crosspool or Stannington, from where there are regular buses to Sheffield city centre.

Maps: A plan of all the watermill sites is shown on page 17, with a more detailed map of the trail inside the back cover. Mini-maps indicating the location of each trail section and each site are given on the relevant pages. Ordnance Survey map Explorer 278 Sheffield & Barnsley, Scale 1:25 000 (2½ in to 1 mile).

Accessibility: Mostly easy walking alongside the river, especially in the first half of the trail from Malin Bridge to Glen Bridge ('S-Bend'). There are some steps and stepping stones in the south-western stretch from Glen Bridge to Rails Road. Paths can become a little muddy after heavy rain. In order to complete the trail, three quite busy roads have to be crossed. The trail is not suitable for mobility scooters. Bicycles and horses are not permitted on the footpaths.

Disabled facilities are available at the toilet block next to the café at **Spooners Wheel**. The Rivelin Water Play area (open during the summer) is accessible to people of all abilities; special aqua wheelchairs are available for loan to disabled children and their carers.

By public transport: The Supertram terminus at Malin Bridge, a 15 minute tram ride from Sheffield city centre, is close to the start of the trail. Malin Bridge is served by more than one regular bus service, but buses along Rivelin Valley Road itself are infrequent.

By car: 10–20 minute drive from Sheffield city centre (depending on traffic). Cars can be parked on Rivelin Valley Road near Malin Bridge, otherwise in small car parks at Havelock Dam and Rails Road. Limited roadside parking by the water play area / café, but roadside parking is not permitted along most of Rivelin Valley Road.

Refreshments: There are pubs, shops and cafés at Hillsborough and Malin Bridge, three pubs close to the trail (The Anvil, near Mousehole Forge; Holly Bush near Hollins Bridge Mill and Rivelin Hotel near Hind Wheel), and a toilet block and café at **Spooners Wheel**. There are plenty of benches and open areas for picnics.

INTRODUCTION

Sheffield was an ideal centre for the development of metal-based industries due to the proximity of iron ore, high quality hard gritstone (for grindstones) and five fast-flowing rivers (Rivelin, Loxley, Don, Sheaf and Porter). These rivers have been used since the twelfth century to power the many waterwheels with their associated mills and workshops that lined the valleys, the products from which helped to secure Sheffield as the world leader in cutlery and fine steels.

The River Rivelin rises high on the heather-clad Hallam Moors on the eastern border of the Peak District National Park to the north-west of Sheffield. The river flows north-eastwards to join the River Loxley at Malin Bridge and then the River Don at Owlerton, reaching the Rivers Ouse and Trent, and finally flowing into the North Sea via the Humber Estuary. The 3½ mile stretch of Rivelin from the Uppermost Mill (in the south-west) to Malin Bridge has a fall in elevation of 280 ft (104 m), with 20 watermills and 21 mill dams (possibly the greatest number over that distance in the country). This guide has been designed to help you trace their remains.

The one remaining building, at Mousehole Forge, has been designated as a Scheduled Ancient Monument (SY1284) by English Heritage and the workshop

The Rivelin Valley, Sheffield.

Fig. 2. View of Rivelin valley in about 1900, looking south-west, with Hind Wheel building and mill dam in the foreground. The Rivelin Hotel can be seen top right. *Sheffield City Council, Libraries Archives and Information: www.picturesheffield.co.uk Image s12144.*

range there is Grade II listed. Four of the bridges along the valley (Hollins Bridge, Roscoe Bridge (Fig. 6), Packhorse Bridge (Fig. 57) and Rivelin Mill Bridge) are also Grade II listed. As well as the historical remains, other features along the route are pointed out, including places to see the flora and fauna and some of the very varied work undertaken by the Rivelin Valley Conservation Group (RVCG) since it was formed in 1991.

The trail route has been printed in **bold type**, so that this can be easily followed, with names of watermill sites shown in blue. A brief historical outline is given for each site and old photographs help to show what the buildings and mill dams looked like in the past. These photographs highlight how much the valley has changed over the years, with woodland now reclaiming areas that were once open. The trail is not waymarked, but there is a cast-iron marker at four of the sites, giving the name and brief details (see page 27). To explore fully all the features noted in this guide, it will be necessary to leave the path at certain points, but please take care not to dislodge any of the remaining stonework or other artefacts.

The Rivelin trail can be enjoyed at all times of the year, but the industrial remains are best seen in winter and early spring when the undergrowth has died back. Late spring and early summer are best for flowering plants and birds, when the dawn chorus is enhanced with summer migrants joining the resident species.

Fig. 3. The trail passes alongside the Havelock Dam (Walkley Bank Tilt mill dam). The open water is maintained for recreational use and is a popular fishing spot. The beech trees along the dam wall provide rich autumnal colours. *Photograph: P. Machin.*

WATER-POWERED INDUSTRY IN RIVELIN

Compared with the other Sheffield rivers, water-power came quite late to Rivelin. **Hind Wheel**, dating from 1581, was the first recorded within the valley, but most were built after 1700. The mills, workshops and forges supported a wide variety of trades (Fig. 5), such as grinding and finishing blades of various types, optical glass grinding, paper making (from rags), corn milling, lead smelting, forging metalwork (including the world-famous anvils from **Mousehole Forge**), wire drawing, making metal strips for ladies corsets, and blacking (see page 40). Generally the watermill sites included other buildings such as storage sheds, stables and dwellings – collectively the buildings are known as a **Wheel**. Most of the Wheels in Rivelin had workshops, known as **hulls**, for grinding and finishing various metal goods including table knives, razors, penknives, saws and fenders. A mill pond is still known locally as a **mill dam**. Most of the Wheels were named after one of their early owners, for example **Spooners, Hind** and **Swallow**. Others are named after their location, as at **Upper Coppice, Hollins Bridge** and **Walkley Bank**.

A painting of the interior of **Holme Head Wheel** (Fig. 4) gives an excellent insight into working conditions here in the mid-19th century. Life in the grinding hulls was tough and unhealthy – often cold and damp and with the air full of stone and metal

Fig. 4. Interior of Holme Head Wheel, Rivelin Valley, Sheffield. Painting by Joseph Wrightson MacIntyre; oil on canvas, 1879. *Courtesy of Museums Sheffield.*

6

Fig. 5. Trades and approximate dates of operation of the Rivelin watermill sites.

Site	Trades at various times
1. Grogram Wheel	Cutlery grinding; bean crushing; lathe; air supply for Mousehole Forge
2. Mousehole Forge	Cutlery grinding; lead mill; iron forge (particularly anvils)
3. Walkley Bank Tilt	Cutlery grinding; tilt forge; wire mill
4. Hollins Bridge Mill	Cutlery grinding; optical glass grinding; corn mill
5. Spooners Wheel	Cutlery, file, saw & scythe grinding
6. New Dam	Water supply for Spooners Wheels; swimming pool
7. Roscoe Wheel	Cutlery, fender & saw grinding; polishing; blacking mill
8. Holme Head Wheel	Grinding (mainly knives & razors)
9. Little London Wheel	Cutlery & file grinding
10. Nether Cut Wheel	Cutlery grinding
11. Upper Cut Wheel	Cutlery grinding; rowing boat hire; swing boats
12. Hind Wheel	Cutlery grinding; making steel strip for ladies corsets
13. Plonk Wheel	Cutlery grinding
14. Swallow Wheel	Cutlery grinding
15. Wolf Wheel	Cutlery & razor grinding
16. Frank Wheel	Cutlery grinding; paper mill
17. Third Coppice Wheel	Cutlery grinding; paper mill
18. Second Coppice Wheel	Cutlery grinding; wire drawing; shops
19. Upper Coppice Wheel	Cutlery grinding; wire drawing
20. Rivelin Corn Mill	Corn mill
21. Uppermost Wheel	Cutlery grinding

7

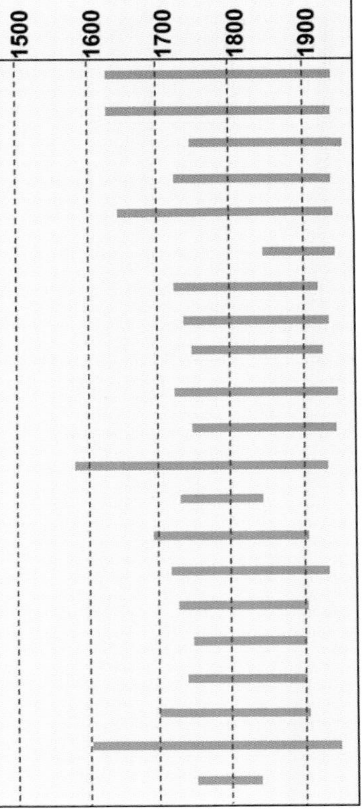

dust, which caused various eye and lung conditions, including silicosis. In the 1830s life expectancy among fork grinders, who used dry grindstones, was around 30 years, whereas table-knife grinders, using wet grindstones, could expect to live to 40 or 50. Other hazards included cracking or even bursting of grindstones. Blade blanks were brought in for the grinders to refine and polish to provide a cutting edge – they were then usually sent to other workshops for handles to be fitted. Each grinder worked at a '**trow**', usually sitting on a wooden seat (**horsin**), which was fastened to the floor with chains, to sharpen the edge of a blade on the grindstone mounted vertically in front of him over a cast-iron trough. Working hours largely depended on daylight, and could be sporadic – for example, work had to stop when water levels were too low to turn the waterwheel in summer, but grinders were expected to remain nearby to resume work when the mill dam refilled. The number of grinding trows in a hull that could be powered depended on the diameter and width of the waterwheel – the largest grinding hull on the Rivelin (**Wolf Wheel**) ran 19 trows from a waterwheel 15 ft in diameter by 6 ft 8 in wide.

In the mid-17th century, there are records of six watermills on the River Rivelin (**Uppermost Wheel, Rivelin Corn Mill, Hind Wheel, Spooners Wheel, Mousehole Forge** and **Grogram** Wheel), owned at that time by the Earls of Shrewsbury. Most of the land in the Rivelin valley-bottom subsequently passed to the Duke of Norfolk Estates, which leased out the land for the building of fourteen more watermills and mill dams, all of which had been built by 1800, with the last, **New Dam**, being built in 1853. The rent for one site was often shared by more than one person, and different parts of the buildings or even individual grinding trows could be sub-let to different tradesmen, or 'Little Mesters', who themselves often employed 'hands'.

In 1848, the Rivelin Dams were built upstream of the **Uppermost Wheel** to impound water from Wyming Brook and the Rivelin in order to supply water for the growing city of Sheffield. An Act of Parliament in 1853 allowed the Sheffield Waterworks Company to purchase the watermills in the Rivelin valley downstream as far as **Walkley Bank Tilt**, *i.e.* all except **Holme Head Wheel** (which was acquired in 1905), **Mousehole Forge** and **Grogram Wheel**. The purchase covered the watermills, mill dams and associated lands, and was primarily to stop any objections to the proposed changes to flows in the River Rivelin, although there was also a requirement to maintain a compensation flow in the Rivelin of 3.25 million gallons per day. Another Act of Parliament in 1887 transferred the Sheffield Waterworks Company to Sheffield Corporation, which took possession of the land in the Rivelin valley on 2nd January 1888. **Mousehole Forge** and **Grogram Wheel** were sold to Sheffield Corporation in 1919, but by 1991 these two sites, as well as **Uppermost Wheel**, were again in private ownership.

As the steel and cutlery industries grew in Sheffield with the advent of steam power and then electricity, the small-scale rural industries were able to move to other areas of the city with better access to the canals and growing road systems. As the

Fig. 6. Roscoe Wheel (left) with cottages adjacent (c. 1900). Roscoe Bridge, now Grade II listed, spans the River Rivelin. *From the KK collection.*

use of waterwheels declined it became harder to lease out the watermills and they became obsolete, quickly falling into decline and disrepair, and many of the buildings were demolished for safety reasons. Nether Cut Wheel was the last to be worked by water power (scythe grinding continued until at least 1939), but Walkley Bank Tilt appears to have been the last in the valley to close, in the early 1950s, although by then it was powered by electricity.

Sheffield Corporation gradually developed parts of the land for allotment gardens and recreation, including the building of a swimming pool at New Dam in 1909, and the playground and paddling pools at Spooners Wheel in the 1950s. The area is now designated as 'Rivelin Valley – City Heritage Park' and is managed and maintained by the Sheffield City Council Parks and Countryside Service, with the assistance of the Rivelin Valley Conservation Group. The latest development was the refurbishment of the paddling pools in 2013 as the Rivelin Valley Water Play (p. 32).

The reference section on page 16 suggests some sources of information on the history of Sheffield water-powered industries and some local museums to visit.

DID YOU KNOW? Records show that there were around 200 men employed at 142 cutlers' trows in the Rivelin valley in 1794.

WEIRS, DAMS, GOITS AND WHEELS

A waterwheel is driven by a flow of water, usually released from a reservoir onto the wheel paddles as needed. The diagram in Fig. 8 represents a river-bypass arrangement, similar to that found at most of the Rivelin sites: a weir deflects river water into a mill dam, from which the water is released to turn the waterwheel, afterwards rejoining the river further downstream.

Almost all of the waterwheels in Rivelin are thought to have been of the **overshot** type, as at **Nether Cut Wheel** (Fig. 7) and **Upper Cut Wheel** (Fig. 40). If there was an insufficient fall of water to run over the top of the waterwheel, a **breast-shot** waterwheel could be used instead (as at **Roscoe Wheel**). None of the waterwheels in Rivelin are thought to have been of the **undershot** type (where the water flows directly across the bottom of the wheel), a restored example of which can be seen on the former Malin Bridge Corn Mill near the start of the trail.

Occasionally, as at **Upper Cut Wheel** and **Nether Cut Wheel**, two sites were run in tandem from only one weir, water from the tail goit of the upper Wheel being fed directly into the head goit/mill dam of the lower Wheel. Several of the sites had two waterwheels (as at Hind Wheel, Fig. 42) and in the early 19th century, there were four waterwheels in operation at **Mousehole Forge,** two overshot and two breast-shot. With so many waterwheels operating along the valley, disagreements

Fig. 7. Pentrough and waterwheel at the derelict Nether Cut Wheel, 1954. The penstock lever can also be seen. *Sheffield City Council, Libraries Archives and Information: www.picturesheffield.co.uk Image y01449.*

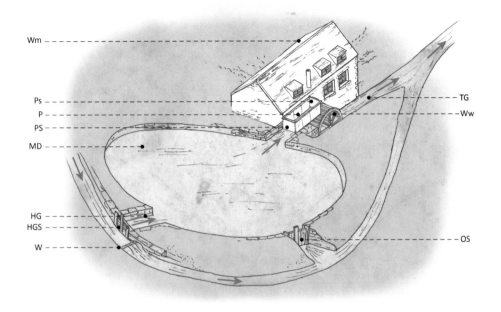

Fig. 8. Diagram of a river-bypass arrangement for delivering a regulated supply of water to turn a waterwheel, which provides the power for grindstones and other machinery.
Drawing: Robbie Ormrod.

A **weir (W)** across a river deflects some of the water through a channel (the **head goit (HG)**) and into the reservoir or mill pond, known locally as a **mill dam (MD)**. The flow of water was usually controlled by a sluice, with a **shuttle (HGS)** (Figs. 9, 28 and 35) that could be raised and lowered by means of a mechanism including a **capstan** and **roller**. Sometimes wooden boards, seated vertically in grooves chiselled into the stonework or placed in metal cleats on top of the stones of the sluice or weir, were used to raise the water level further.

One or more **waterwheels (Ww)** and associated **watermill (Wm)** buildings were located at the downstream end of the dam, where operation of another shuttle (**PS**) allowed water from the mill dam to flow into a narrow trough called the **pentrough (P)** (Fig. 7). From here, the flow of water onto the waterwheel could be controlled from the adjacent building by levers operating the **penstock (Ps)**. The rotating waterwheel powered the main drive shaft – power being taken off this shaft inside the building by a series of gears and subsidiary drive shafts in order to turn the grindstones or to operate other machinery, such as hammers and hoists.

Below the waterwheel the water flowed along another channel (the **tail goit (TG)**) to rejoin the river downstream. An **overflow** sluice (**OS**) along the side of the mill dam, controlled by another shuttle and/or boards, prevented the dam from over-filling and a low drainage level acted as a point from where water could be drained from the dam for maintenance.

between neighbours over maintaining an adequate water supply for all were not uncommon. After the building of the Rivelin Dams in 1848 (see page 8), there were also disputes with Sheffield Waterworks Company. In 1866, when the Company proposed to increase the amount of water taken from the river to supply the city, the dispute involving the occupiers of **Mousehole Forge** even ended up in Parliament, with a Select Committee set up to hear the arguments for both sides!

The mill dams in the Rivelin valley were about 1.5–3 m deep, lined with puddled clay to hold in the water. The mill dams were kept clear of vegetation and could usually be drained for maintenance through a low-level shuttle on the overflow.

The length of the head goit and tail goit at each watermill depended on the fall on the river and the height of water needed to turn the waterwheel. A particular problem was achieving the correct level of outfall into the river at the end of the tail goit, as there was a need to avoid water backing up the channel when river levels were high, which could prevent the waterwheel from turning. In sites where the floor of the wheel pit was below the level of the river (in order to increase the size of waterwheel that could be run), it was necessary to separate the tail goit from the river by building a low dividing wall downstream to a point where the water levels were equal – examples of this arrangement can be seen at **Hollins Bridge Mill, Holme Head Wheel** and **Third Coppice Wheel.**

Fig. 9. Shuttle mechanism on the head goit entry at Upper Cut weir (river on left, head goit on right) (undated). The capstan and roller can still be seen. *Sheffield City Council, Libraries Archives and Information: www.picturesheffield.co.uk Image s12275.*

HABITATS AND WILDLIFE

Over the last 300 million years, the upper reaches of the Rivelin valley have been carved out of the sandstones, mudstones and shales of the Millstone Grit. There are many old quarries in the area from where millstones and grindstones were hewn from the hard gritstone. In the lower reaches (to the NE of the junction of Hagg Hill with Rivelin Valley Road, and on the valley sides) the Millstone Grit dips beneath the Pennine Lower Coal Measures Formation. Between approximately **Wolf Wheel** and Malin Bridge the bedrock is capped by Alluvium (gravel, sand, silt and clay), and there is a small area of 'Head' (downwashed debris) near **Upper Cut Wheel/Hind Wheel**. At many points in the valley rusty-coloured water can be seen seeping out of the ground – this is natural and due to iron in the water draining through iron-rich mineral deposits oxidising when it comes into contact with the air.

Alder

Ash

With the gradual demise of the mills since the mid-19th century, the valley bottom has been slowly reclaimed by nature and is now a haven for wildlife – much of it (excluding allotments) has been designated as a "Site of Interest for Nature Conservation" by Sheffield City Council. Backed by rocky edges, the steeper slopes on the valley sides are mainly natural woodland and heath, while the gentler slopes are mostly pasture. Apart from the river itself, the main habitat along the valley bottom and river-side slopes is woodland, but there is also a wide variety of other habitats, including mill dams, streams, river cliffs, waterfalls, grassland, parkland, allotments, old walls and hedges. The silting-up and overgrowth of many mill dams provides some interesting examples of succession from open water to dry land.

Beech

The most common **trees** are Alder (or Owler tree, from which is derived the local name Owlerton – the settlement of the Alders), Ash, Oak, Sycamore and Willow, with others such as Beech, Birch, Bird Cherry, Elder, Wych Elm, Hawthorn, Hazel, Hornbeam, Rowan, Whitebeam and Wild Cherry. Many of the trees and some of the banks are overgrown with Ivy. Holly is also common, although seemingly never with many berries here. Holly has the local name of Hollin, which can be found in some local place names (*e.g.* Hollins Lane); the term can also refer to stands of trees, hollins or holly haggs, where the soft, spikeless upper leaves of holly were cut as winter fodder for sheep and cattle.

Holly

Oak

There is also an interesting **herbaceous flora** within the woodland, alongside the river and within the overgrown mill dams. Species to look for, particularly in spring and early summer, include Bluebell, Brooklime, Celandine, Cow Parsley, Dog's Mercury, Enchanter's Nightshade, Foxglove, Great Woodrush, Greater Stitchwort, Herb Bennett, Herb Robert, Nettle, Pendulous Sedge, Ramsons, Stitchwort, Violet, Wood Anemone, Wood Sorrel and Yellow Archangel. In wet places, especially within the revegetating mill dams, plants found include Figwort, Flote Grass, Forget-me-not, Great Hairy Willowherb, Iris, Marsh Marigold, Opposite-leaved Golden Saxifrage, Reedmace, Water Mint and Woundwort. Water Horsetail can be seen at several mill dams along the valley – it was a constant problem to the mill owners, who employed men to rake out the mill dams on a regular basis. Ferns, mosses and liverworts also thrive in the damp, shady conditions throughout the valley.

In addition to the native plants, there are several naturalised 'alien' plants (**garden escapes**) in the valley. Himalayan Balsam is an invasive annual, reaching 2–3 m in height, which produces clusters of purplish pink (sometimes white) helmet-shaped flowers between June and October. It is particularly common on riverbanks and has spread the whole length of the Rivelin trail since the 1960s. It was introduced to gardens from the Himalayas in 1839, first recorded in the wild in Britain in 1855, and has increased rapidly throughout the country in recent decades. Other naturalised 19th century garden escapes include Monkeyflower, the yellow flowers of which can be seen around Malin Bridge and at **Hollins Bridge Mill**, and Pink Purslane, found mainly from **Hind Wheel** to **Upper Coppice Wheel**.

There are still several areas of working **allotments** along the valley, but there were once many more. Abandoned allotments can be traced particularly by the presence of overgrown Privet bushes, as well as the remains of walls and other structures.

A wide variety of **birds** can be seen and heard along the valley, including woodland species such as Great Spotted Woodpecker, Nuthatch, Siskin, Treecreeper (Fig. 41), and summer migrants such as Blackcap, Chiffchaff, Willow Warbler and Wood

Fig. 10. Long-tailed Tit (left) and Kingfisher (right) are regularly seen along the Rivelin valley. *Photographs: Andy Jones*

Warbler. Other species regularly seen are Blackbird, Chaffinch, Grey Wagtail (Fig. 41), Goldcrest, Magpie, Robin, Thrush, and Wren (Fig. 39), as well as several species of tit: Blue, Coal, Great, Long-tailed and Willow. The populations of Long-tailed Tits (Fig. 10) have been the subject of a long-term scientific study by the University of Sheffield since 1994. Dippers (Fig. 39) are often seen along the river, with occasional sightings of Kingfisher (Fig. 10) and Heron (Fig. 41). A visit at dawn or dusk may be rewarded with the sight of a Tawny or Barn Owl. Sparrowhawks are regularly seen in the area, as well as Buzzard, Kestrel and occasionally a Red Kite.

The mill dams are home to **amphibians**, including frogs, toads and newts, and breeding **water-bird** species such as Coot, Mallard and Moorhen. **Dragonflies** such as the Common Darter and the Common Hawker are sometimes seen skimming the surface. Stickleback, tadpoles, freshwater shrimps and snails, Greater Diving Beetle, Hoglouse, Leech, Limpet, Water Boatman, Water Flea, and the larvae of Alderfly, Caddisfly, Mayfly and Stonefly can all be found in the mill dams and river.

A few of the mill dams are used for fishing, with regular catches of **fish** species such as Trout and Perch. Brown Trout can also be found in the river, as well as other fish species such as Bullhead, Brook Lamprey and Stone Loach. A recent unwelcome addition is the American Signal Crayfish, an invasive non-native **crustacean** species that presents a significant risk to native wildlife and is now increasing in numbers rapidly in waterways throughout England.

Butterflies are mainly found around the allotments and open grassy areas, and include Brimstone, Comma (Fig. 11), Gate Keeper, Holly Blue, Orange-tip (the first to appear in spring, Fig. 11) , Painted Lady, Peacock and Speckled Wood (Fig. 45).

Apart from Grey Squirrels (an introduced American species that replaced the native Red Squirrel here in about 1954), which are often seen throughout the valley, **mammals** are seldom seen. Species noted include Badger, Fox and Weasel. Be on

Fig. 11. Orange-tip (left) and Comma (right) butterflies are usually amongst the first to appear in spring. *Photographs: Andy Jones.*

the look-out in the mud along the trail for the spoor of Roe or Muntjac deer, which are increasing in numbers in this area. Although not reported for many years, Water Voles may still be present. On summer evenings bats, including Daubenton's, Noctule and Pipistrelle can be seen along the valley, especially around the grassy areas, along the river and over the mill dams.

The RVCG keeps wildlife records and welcomes details of local sightings, which can be submitted via the RVCG website.

Further reading and information

A History of Sheffield. David Hey (2010). Carnegie Publishing.

Mousehole Forge. Richard A. Postman with John and Julia Hatfield (2003). Postma Publishing.

Reminiscing around Rivelin. Roy Davey (2005). DS Publishing.

The water-mills of Sheffield. W.T. Miller (1936). 4th edition (1949). Sheffield Trades Historical Society.

Water Power on the Sheffield Rivers. C. Ball, D. Crossley, N. Flavell (Editors). 2nd Edition (2006). South Yorkshire Industrial Society.

Where t'watter runs o'er t' weir. A look back at Sheffield's Watermills. Roy Davey (2008). DS Publishing.

'**Picture Sheffield**'. Images of Sheffield from Sheffield City Council's Local Studies Library. Website: www.picturesheffield.com/index.php

Rivelin Valley Conservation Group. Website: www.rivelinvalley.org.uk

Where to see more of Sheffield's Industrial heritage

Abbeydale Industrial Hamlet: an 18th century rural scythe and steelworks on the River Sheaf. *South-west Sheffield.*

Kelham Island Museum: objects, pictures and archive material representing Sheffield's industrial story, including a 'Little Mesters Street' and the working 'River Don' steam engine. *Central Sheffield.*

Shepherd Wheel: a restored 18th century waterwheel and grinding shop in the Porter Valley. *South-west Sheffield.*

Wortley Top Forge: 17th Century Iron Forge, the oldest surviving heavy iron forge in the world. *North of Sheffield, near Stocksbridge.*

Watermills of the Rivelin Valley

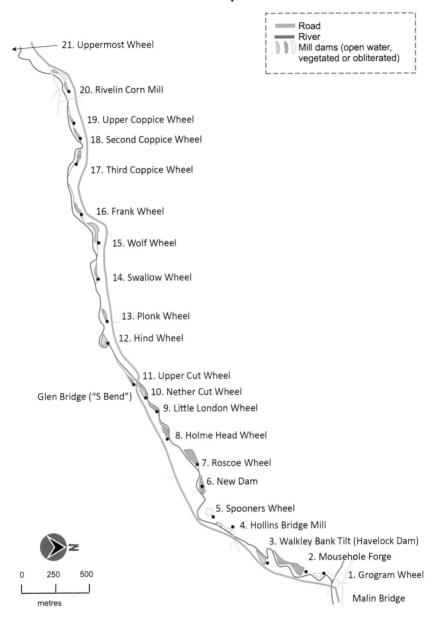

Road
River
Mill dams (open water, vegetated or obliterated)

21. Uppermost Wheel

20. Rivelin Corn Mill

19. Upper Coppice Wheel

18. Second Coppice Wheel

17. Third Coppice Wheel

16. Frank Wheel

15. Wolf Wheel

14. Swallow Wheel

13. Plonk Wheel

12. Hind Wheel

11. Upper Cut Wheel

Glen Bridge ("S Bend")   10. Nether Cut Wheel

9. Little London Wheel

8. Holme Head Wheel

7. Roscoe Wheel

6. New Dam

5. Spooners Wheel

4. Hollins Bridge Mill

3. Walkley Bank Tilt (Havelock Dam)

2. Mousehole Forge

1. Grogram Wheel

Malin Bridge

N

0   250   500

metres

MALIN BRIDGE TO RIVELIN PARK CAFÉ

Distance: 1.4 km; 0.85 mile

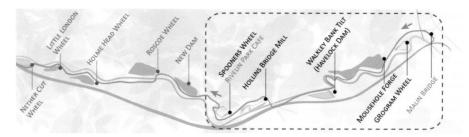

MALIN BRIDGE

The trail starts on Rivelin Valley Road on the 'New Bridge' over the River Loxley (Fig. 12). The bridge was built when the Rivelin Valley Road was constructed in 1905–8 (see page 77). Look west (upstream) from here to see the confluence of the River Rivelin (to the left) and River Loxley (flowing under the bridge to the right). The low weir across the Rivelin deflects river water through an open channel and into the Loxley just above the Loxley weir. The combined waters then pass into the small mill dam to your right (next to Holme Lane). This stored the water to power the waterwheel at the mill behind you, La Plata Works, now occupied by Burgon & Ball, specialist makers of sheep-shears and cutting tools since the 1870s.

In 2011, the banks were cleared of mature trees and vegetation and the river bed was re-formed to allow flood water to pass more freely under the bridge. The banks are slowly being recolonised naturally by shrubs and trees, including Alder, Willow and Buddleja ('Butterfly Bush') with its purple flowers in summer. Dippers (Fig. 39) and Grey Wagtails (Fig. 41) can often be seen feeding in the shallows.

On the night of 11 March 1864, Malin Bridge was hit by the Great Sheffield Flood, one of the worst man-made disasters in British history (apart from wars). About 5 miles upstream (just above Low Bradfield), the newly-built wall of the Dale Dyke mill dam collapsed, releasing a huge amount of water which swept down the Loxley valley. More than 600 houses were damaged or destroyed and of the 240 people who died that night, 96 were from Malin Bridge.

The building to the right of the bridge opposite is the former Malin Bridge Corn Mill, one of the mills that were destroyed that night. **Follow the wall around the river and walk towards the mill. Cross Stannington Road to look at the restored waterwheel on the side of the mill building.** This undershot waterwheel was restored in the 1970s, and is not typical of the waterwheels that powered the

Rivelin valley watermills, which were mainly overshot or breastshot. There is no mill dam – water reaches the waterwheel via a short head goit separated from the river by a wall; the tail goit outfall into the river is beneath the road bridge.

Walk up Stannington Road for about 50 metres and cross the road again at the pedestrian crossing. Look over the wall here and down at the river – the end of the tail goit from Grogram Wheel is visible directly below the wall, marked by a wide concrete slab. **Turn right and then take the Public Bridleway (Easy Going Trail) that heads off to the left.** Along this stretch of the trail, look out for some of the most common trees in the valley: Alder, Ash, Crack Willow, Elder, Goat Willow and Sycamore.

Follow the path, passing a metal fence that surrounds an electricity substation – this stands on the site of one of the largest waterwheels (Fig. 13) **that used to run in the valley, at** GROGRAM WHEEL [1]. On the open bank to the right can be seen a variety of common wild flowers such as Cow Parsley, Cleavers, Herb Bennett, Herb Robert and White Deadnettle. **Just past the end of the metal fence, walk down onto the river bank on the left to look at the** Grogram **weir.** Water from here was culverted under the bank and directly into the Grogram mill dam (behind you). The weir is just about all that is left of this Wheel (Fig. 16), which used to attract visitors from all over the country. Look closely at the river bank and island and you will see discarded molten metal (from the nearby forge) that has solidified over the rocks.

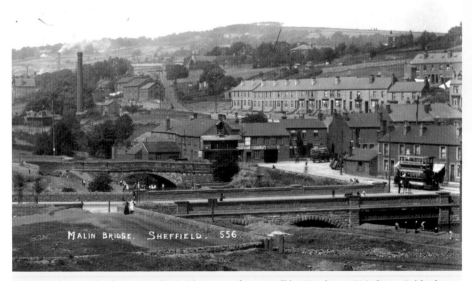

Fig. 12. The two bridges at Malin Bridge, seen from Walkley Bank, *c.* 1912. 'New Bridge', built in 1905–8, is in the foreground, and the bridge over the River Loxley behind with Malin Bridge Corn Mill to its right. *From the KK collection.*

GROGRAM WHEEL (c. 1620s–1935)

Map reference: SK 3251 8919
Also known as: Groggerham Wheels, Saw Mill.
Main trades: Grinding cutlery, files, sickles, anvils & hammers; bean crushing; lathe; air supply for Mousehole Forge furnaces.

Dating from the 1620s (or perhaps before), Grogram Wheel was amongst the earliest to be built in the valley. The two workshops each had a waterwheel – these were located next to each other between the two buildings (Fig. 16). The larger of the two (Fig. 13), known affectionately as the 'Groggie' amongst the locals, was said to be the largest waterwheel in the valley and at one time ran 12 cutler's trows; the smaller waterwheel ran six trows.

The Grogram Wheel and its much larger upstream neighbour, the Mousehole Forge, were purchased in 1842 by Henry Armitage from Lady Burgoyne for £2,100. Records show that in 1852, Grogram was grinding (finishing) anvils and hammers, and had a lathe, bean crusher and blowing apparatus. In the mid-19th century, the larger Grogram waterwheel was used to supply extra air for the furnaces at Mousehole Forge, the two sites being connected by large cast-iron pipes. The close proximity of the two sites is evident in Fig. 16, which shows Grogram in the foreground, with the larger Mousehole complex behind. The photograph in Fig. 14 shows workers in the mid-19th century.

Being the closest to Malin Bridge, the Grogram waterwheels were the only ones in Rivelin to be damaged by the Great Sheffield Flood of 1864, when water backed-up on the Rivelin due to the flood water in the River Loxley at Malin Bridge (see page 18). The claim for damage and stoppage, including wages for clearing up and repairs, amounted to £440 4s 4d (although only £170 was allowed). The 'Groggie' ceased to operate around 1933 and the main building was demolished in 1935 (Fig. 15). The waterwheel was reported to be in ruins in 1949.

The weir, a short, blocked head goit and the outfall from the tail goit into the river are all that remains. The wide weir is in fair condition. Its design is unusual – the southern section is curved and is a typical block-stone slope, but on the northern side the river cascades over a straight, vertical stone wall. The river bank and island here are coated in discarded molten metal, waste material from the nearby Mousehole Forge, that has solidified over the rocks. There is an electricity sub-station on the site of the mill dam.

DID YOU KNOW? Grinding was very skilled work and grinders were some of the best paid workers in Sheffield.

Fig. 13. The larger of the two Grogram waterwheels, in 1934. The original was damaged by the Sheffield flood of 1864. *From Miller, 1936.*

Fig. 14. Grinders from Mousehole Forge and Grogram Wheel, possibly taken after winning gold at the Great Exhibition at Crystal Palace in 1851. *From the KK collection.*

Just upstream of the weir at the bottom of the wall to the right, two arches mark where the Mousehole Forge tail goits flow into the river. There is a large Wych Elm on the river bank here, as well as Alder, Hawthorn and Sycamore.

Return to the path and keep left on the track to arrive at the gates of the MOUSEHOLE FORGE [2]. Of all the Rivelin mill sites, Mousehole probably had the largest number of buildings (Fig. 16). Most have now gone, but the house, a few warehouses and some of the best remains of a forge in the valley have been lovingly rescued and restored by the owners. The site is designated as a Scheduled Ancient Monument (SY1284) and the workshop range is also Grade II listed. Mousehole Forge is on private land, but some of the forge remains can still be seen from outside the gates. The huge oak log, over 22 ft long by nearly 3 ft in diameter, is the remains of a hammer helve. In the mid-18th century, the forge was operated by the same ironmaster (John Cockshutt) as at Wortley Top Forge (on the River Don near Stocksbridge, now a museum). In the early 19th century, the Armitage family, partners at Mousehole Forge, built Wood Lane House (now the Countryside Centre) nearby on Wood Lane at Stannington.

On leaving the Mousehole Forge, continue on the bridleway to the Mousehole/Racker Way bridge (once part of the main thoroughfare up to Walkley and Sheffield city centre). This old stone bridge was built in the late 18th century by William Armitage of Mousehole Forge to replace a ford. Look across the river to the wall alongside the road – the two gates in the wall are 'snow-gates', where snow from the road could be shovelled directly into the river. **Keep right and walk**

AFTER 200 YEARS

Sheffield Water Wheel to be Destroyed.

DAMAGE BY CHILDREN.

Damage to the 200 years old Grogram water wheel at Malin Bridge, Sheffield, by children trespassing over the ancient fabric has resulted in its forced demolition.

The Grogram water wheel is one of the oldest bits of Sheffield. Some people believe it to be the finest water wheel in the Rivelin Valley. Certainly, it is one of the biggest in Sheffield.

For some time, the Grogam wheel, with its adjoining buildings, has been Corporation property. To prevent trespass, a great deal of barbed wire was placed round and over the building, but to no avail.

Building Roof Falls In.

On Wednesday morning of this week, the roof gave way and fell in debris. Fortunately, no children were playing round the building at the time and no one was hurt.

By co-incidence, the man who witnessed this fall was Mr. Walter Gregory, who, until two years ago, when the wheel ceased to operate, had worked in the building for 45 years.

Corporation officials decided that nothing could be done to save the building. There-fore, yesterday afternoon saw the main building pulled down in one solid mass.

But the Grogram wheel was undisturbed ; the water still flowed round it.

Adjoining the demolished building is another workshop—this occupied by Mr. W. Hancock, who there manufactures surgical instruments. This building is now unsafe and it will be a matter of only a few days before it is pulled down and Mr. Hancock loses his manufacturing home.

The Doomed "Groggie."

When the Grogram wheel is to be destroyed has not been determined. But there is little doubt of its imminent departure, because of its unsafe condition.

An interested spectator of the demolitiion operations yesterday was Mr. S. V. Peace, secretary of the Rivelin Valley Protection Society.

"The Corporation have done their best to preserve this ancient bit of Sheffield." He said. "People have come from miles to see this wheel, which is known familiarly as 'Groggie.' It is a perfect wheel, a beautiful wheel."

Fig. 15. Article from the Sheffield Star, dated August 1935, describing the demolition of Grogram Wheel.

down the path onto the river bank. On the right are the largely overgrown remains of the mill dam that used to feed the waterwheels at the Mousehole Forge. Here you can still get a feel for the scale of what was one of the largest mill dams in the valley. It is now largely dry, and has been well-colonised by trees such as Ash, Alder, Elder, Sycamore, Holly, Hawthorn, Elm and Willow since the forge closed in the 1930s; at the time of writing (2014), there is a large amount of the invasive species Himalayan Balsam here.

By the side of the path about 100 m from the bridge are the massive stone remains of the overflow sluice for the Mousehole Forge mill dam, a good example of a double-overflow with a central draining hatch. Water flowed over on both sides of the central structure, down the hatch in the middle and then under the path and into the river. Look for the grooves in the top stones for the wooden boards that were used to raise the water level. The ironworks on the central stones are part of the shuttle mechanism that controlled water flow at the low drainage level – this was opened when it was necessary to drain the mill dam for maintenance.

Continue on this footpath to a wooden bridge. Just to the right of the bridge is a large Wild Cherry (or Gean) tree, with horizontally-striped bark and white flowers in spring followed by red, cherry-like fruit. **Cross the river and turn right to follow the river bank.** This way you will pass the Mousehole weir, from which water was directed into the Mousehole mill dam – the head goit entry is marked by the large stone blocks on the bank opposite. There are several large Oaks at the top of the steep wooded bank opposite, which is a favourite early morning haunt for the Great Spotted Woodpecker. Brambles, ferns, ivy and liverworts grow on the damp rocky outcrop. Watch out for a Kingfisher (Fig. 10) on this stretch of the river.

Fig. 16. Artist's impression of Mousehole Forge in the early 19th century , as it stood in its heyday. Grogram Wheel and mill dam are in the foreground. *Courtesy J. Hatfield & R. Postman.*

23

MOUSEHOLE FORGE (c. 1620s–1930s)

Map reference: SK 3246 8905

Main trades: Lead mill (smelting), cutlers' forge, iron forge (iron bars, vice-legs, sledgehammers, anvils).

The history of **Mousehole Forge** dates back to at least 1628, when the land was called Turneholme & Leyes Stubbing and there are records of two lead mills ('smelting houses'). At this time there was a farmhouse (part of the present house) which incorporated a small cutlery workshop. By 1664 the lead mill had been converted into an iron forge. This was included in the national list of ironworks in 1717, at which time the annual production of iron bars amounted to some 60 tons, converted from blast furnace pig-iron.

By the end of the 18th century the forge was producing the anvils for which it became famous throughout the world. It was one of the leading exporters to the USA and hundreds of **Mousehole Forge** anvils, much sought after by collectors, are still available there. The anvils won much acclaim and were awarded a gold medal at the 1851 Great Exhibition at Crystal Palace. One of the anvils at Gretna Green bears the mark of **Mousehole Forge** (see Fig. 17).

In the early 19th century, three more waterwheels were built, giving a total of four: two breast-shot wheels powering forge hammers, and two overshot wheels powering a furnace-blower and grindstones for finishing anvils. Extra air for the furnaces was supplied via cast-iron pipes from the **Grogram Wheel** in the mid-19th century, which meant that more water was available at Mousehole to power the hammers and grinding wheel. An artist's impression of the site at around this time is shown in Fig. 16.

Along with vice-legs and sledgehammers, anvils were made using water-powered hammers until 1933, when the forge closed. Parts were demolished in the 1940s and the site fell into ruin until the 1980s, after which some of the best remains of a forge to be seen in the valley were restored by the owners.

The remnants of the former forge complex, along with parts of the surviving timber belly-helve hammer and a puddling furnace, are considered to be of national significance – the site is designated as a Scheduled Ancient Monument (SY1284) and the workshop range is also Grade II listed.

The weir, made of stone blocks, is slightly curved and still in good condition. Large stone blocks mark the entry to the short head goit, which now leads into a shallow channel along the bottom of the steep hillslope. The drained mill dam is well wooded. The massive stone blocks that are the remains of the overflow sluice can be seen by the side of the trail – this is a good example of a double-overflow with a central draining hatch. Water from the overflow was culverted beneath the path and out into the river through an arch in the stone-work. The tail goits are culverted under the path and flow into the river through arches in the river wall just above the **Grogram** weir. There is also said to have been a third, more recent culvert.

The book 'Mousehole Forge' by Postman, Hatfield & Hatfield gives details of the history of the forge and its products as well as its restoration. It includes the following rhyme by Joseph Senior (1819–92):

"And yonder stands old Mousehole Forge
In dingy honours dres't,
Famed in the days of good King George
For anvils, England's best."

SAVING RIVELIN—3

GRETNA ANVIL BEARS STAMP OF MOUSEHOLE

IN this final article on Rivelin Valley, it is proposed to deal with some of the wheels and mills which have a special historic interest, and which, more than all others, should be preserved.

First, however, it should be appreciated that virtually all the wheels and mills in the valley were built about the same time, more than 200 years ago, and that many of them were worked by successive generations of the same families until closed in recent years.

Perhaps the most famous of the water wheels in the valley is the Mousehole Forge, which stands close to Malin Bridge.

For centuries, Mousehole Forge was regarded as a typical example of a Sheffield industry and was one of the most famous forges in the world. To-day there are many pictures in existence of the forge as it was years ago.

Anvils were made at Mousehole Forge, reputed to be the finest anvils in the world, because of the exceptional hardening qualities of the River Rivelin. These anvils were exported to all parts of the globe and the anvil in the old Smithy at Gretna Green bears the mark of Mousehole Forge.

Fig. 17. Mousehole Forge and the Gretna anvil. *An article from the Sheffield Star around 1936.*

WALKLEY BANK TILT (c. 1750s–1950s)

Map reference: SK 3242 8881
Also known as: Hallam Wheel, Havelock Steel & Wire Mills, Walkley Tilt.
[Havelock Dam]
Main trades: Cutlery grinding, tilt forge, wire-drawing mill.

The Church Burgesses of Sheffield owned the land on which Walkley Bank Tilt stood. Its history as a cutlers' Wheel can be traced back as far as 1751 (when it was noted as 'newly built'), but in 1762 Jonathan Parker & William Hawksworth purchased the lease and converted it to a tilt-forge* (Fig. 18). A valuation of this forge in 1812 included a sketch showing the overshot waterwheel. In 1831 a 42-year lease was taken up by Joseph Oakes & Joseph Hawksworth, but by 1865 the Sheffield Waterworks Company had bought the property and Moss & Gamble (a well-known Sheffield name) were the tenants.

Around 1897, the tilt-forge was converted to a wire-drawing mill, operated by George Hallam & Co, who later installed an oil engine (although records show that the waterwheel was still capable of use in 1916). Electric power came to the Walkley Bank Tilt in the 1920s and the mill was the last in the valley to close, in the early 1950s. Fig. 20 shows the mill and dam in the early 20th century.

The weir is in good condition, having undergone some repairs; a modern shuttle gate has been installed on the head goit entry. The open water of the mill dam is now maintained for recreational use. Most of the buildings stood between the mill dam and the Mousehole weir, but few traces of the once-thriving mill now remain. The outfall from the short tail goit is close to the Mousehole weir, the exit from the forge building marked by a bricked-up stone arch halfway between the mill dam and the weir.

A tilt hammer is pivoted like a see-saw – a cam mechanism pushes the tail end down, thereby raising the hammer end, then releases so that the hammer falls by gravity. A rapid stroke rate could be achieved, making tilt hammers suitable for drawing iron down to small sizes suitable for the Sheffield cutlery trades.

The bricked-up stone arch to the left of the path just above the Mousehole weir marks the remains of the tail goit from the next site, WALKLEY BANK TILT (Havelock Dam) [3]. **Follow the path around the river bank (without crossing the stepping stones) and up the slope to the mill dam.** This is one of four mill dams along the valley where open water is maintained for recreational use, and is a popular fishing spot. Look out for the cast-iron mill marker (Fig. 19) commissioned by the RVCG and designed by Sheffield sculptor Roger Gibson to represent various aspects of the valley – a wheel is mounted on a plinth that depicts a seed-pod emerging from the

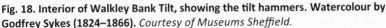

Fig. 18. Interior of Walkley Bank Tilt, showing the tilt hammers. Watercolour by Godfrey Sykes (1824–1866). *Courtesy of Museums Sheffield.*

ground, with flowing water cascading downwards over weirs. There are four markers in the valley: the marker here depicts a scythe blade, the marker at Hind Wheel a fork (page 49), that at Third Coppice Wheel a spoon (page 69) and at Rivelin Corn Mill an ear of corn (page 73).

Turn right to follow the footpath between the mill dam and the river. The metal plate across the path marks the overflow from the mill dam to the river. The RVCG has installed benches around the dam and at least once every two years the encroaching vegetation is cut back to keep it clear for the fishermen. On a beautiful autumn afternoon there can be nothing finer than to sit watching the birds and enjoying the rich colours of the turning leaves of the huge Beech trees along the dam wall (Fig. 3). This is one of the few places where Coot, Mallard and Moorhen all nest successfully – May/June is a good time to

Fig. 19. Cast iron mill marker at Walkley Bank Tilt (Havelock Dam), installed by RVCG in 2002.

see the chicks and spot the differences between them. The open water is partly colonised by Water Horsetails, and Weeping Willows on the far bank skim the water surface. The wide and shallow stretch of river below the dam is popular with Grey Wagtails (Fig. 41).

Follow the path along the dam wall to cross the head goit at a stone bridge, with the Walkley Bank Tilt weir to your right. The stone steps by the river just above the weir were probably a fishing platform. To the left of the path are some shrubs, including Dogwood, Laurel and Wild Cherry, that were probably planted.

After about 100 m, walk up the slope towards Rivelin Valley Road. Near the top of the slope, look up the river to see the remains of the tail goit from Hollins Bridge Mill – a series of stone slabs along the north side of the river, joined by metal staples. Another good view of the tail goit can be seen if you look down to the river as you **turn right onto Rivelin Valley Road and right again to cross the early 19th century, Grade II listed Hollins Bridge.** A Police Box used to stand here on the corner of Rivelin Valley Road (on the upstream side of the bridge) balancing precariously over the river. It stood empty for a long time but it was inevitable that one day it would be hit by a car and knocked into the river – which it was!

Just after you cross the bridge, there is a multi-trunked Bird Cherry tree on your right – this has white flowers in spring and dark purple/black cherry-like fruits in autumn. **Cross the road (Hollins Lane) and join the path again with the river now on your left. Here stood the fourth site along the valley, HOLLINS BRIDGE MILL [4].**

Continue on the path to pass a long weir (Fig. 23). This was built in the early 1900s when the course of the river was altered to flow through **Hollins Bridge Mill** dam (Fig. 24). The large stone structure beside the weir is probably the remains of the intake / shuttle for the wheel pit.

The **RIVELIN VALLEY WATER PLAY** area (see page 32) is on the far bank and on the grassy bank to the right are several old Ash and Oak trees. **Walk along to the café** and near the next weir also look out for a Weeping Willow, two Rowan trees and tall pines, and in summer at the river's edge, the yellow flowers of the Monkey-flower.

When the river level is low, the water inlets for the original paddling pools can be seen at the bottom of the wall just above the weir. The large 'ruler' (gauge board) fixed to the wall here is used by the Environment Agency to monitor water levels in the river.

DID YOU KNOW? The original Rivelin paddling pools were built in the 1950s as part of the Festival of Britain. They were fed directly by water from the river.

Fig. 20. Walkley Bank Tilt and mill dam (Havelock Dam), taken from Walkley Bank in the early 20th century. The buildings immediately behind are on Stannington Road, with The Anvil pub far left. *Sheffield City Council, Libraries Archives and Information: www.picturesheffield.co.uk Image t06402.*

Fig. 21. Extract from 1864 map showing the original location of Chadburn Wheel (Hollins Bridge Mill) and reservoir (mill dam) before the river was diverted. Spooners Wheel (unnamed) and mill dam are to the left. *Sheffield City Council, Libraries Archives and Information: Sheffield Archives ACM/SP/56: ACM (Arundel Castle Manuscripts) reproduced with permission from His Grace the Duke of Norfolk, DL and the Director of Culture, Sheffield City Council.*

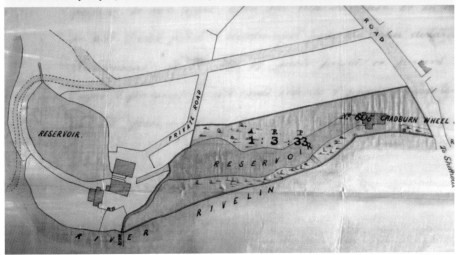

HOLLINS BRIDGE MILL (1720s–1930s)

Map reference: SK 3219 8849
Also known as: Chadburn Wheel, Hollins Bridge Corn Mill, Rivelin Bridge Wheel.
Main trades: Grinding cutlery, fenders and optical glass; corn mill.

Hollins Bridge Mill was erected around 1724, and had six grinding trows. In 1794 Hague & Parkin employed nine men here. 20 years later, in 1814, the number of trows had increased to one fender trow, seven cutlers' trows and an unknown number of glass trows, the latter being used by Chadburns for the grinding of optical glass lenses for use in glasses and telescopes. In 1860, the Wheel was sold to Sheffield Waterworks Company; by 1868 it had been converted to a corn mill and in about 1909 was being run by John Wilson, the owner of the Malin Bridge Corn Mill. It was noted in 1936 as being "little used".

Despite having the old map (Fig. 21), photograph (Fig. 22) and drawing (Fig. 23), it is now quite hard to imagine what this area was like when the Wheel was in operation. The course of the river originally ran through what is now the Rivelin Water Play area, being separated from the mill dam by a narrow embankment. A weir across the river, approximately in the location of the current bridge by the toilet block, deflected water into the mill dam. In the early 20th century, around the time the 'New Road' was built along the valley, the river was diverted to flow directly through the former mill dam. The difference in the height of water was preserved by a new weir (Fig. 23), which is one of the longest weirs in the valley. The water level could be raised further by inserting wooden boards into metal cleats on the top of the weir – remains of four of these cleats can still be seen. The width of the river at this point meant that raising the water level could increase considerably the amount of water available to turn the waterwheel. There were further changes in this area when the paddling pools were built in 1951.

The remains of the tail goit can still be seen under Hollins Bridge, joining the river on the downstream side of the bridge via a channel separated from the river by a series of stone slabs. This arrangement was needed to equalise the water levels in the tail goit and river to prevent water backing up the tail goit when river levels were high (which would prevent the waterwheel from turning). A similar stone wall can be seen on the tail goits at Holme Head Wheel and Third Coppice Wheel.

DID YOU KNOW? Rivelin Valley Road was built between 1905 and 1908 from Malin Bridge to the Sheffield–Glossop turnpike road (now A57 Manchester Road) near Rivelin Corn Mill. Before this there was no through-route along the valley bottom.

Fig. 22. Hollins Bridge Mill and mill dam, before the course of the river was changed (undated). *Sheffield City Council, Libraries Archives and Information: www.picturesheffield.co.uk Image u01693.*

Fig. 23. Drawing of Hollins Bridge Mill by Mr A. Chattle. The weir was built in the early 20th century when the course of the river was changed. *Courtesy of M. Chattle.*

OLD FLOUR MILL
HOLLINS BRIDGE, RIVELIN

A. CHATTLE

31

Fig. 24. Hollins Bridge Mill dam after diversion of the river into the mill dam in the early 20th century. The original paddling pools (now the 'Rivelin Valley Water Play') were built on the land on the right of the picture. *From the KK collection.*

RIVELIN PLAY AREAS

Rivelin Valley Park, including the children's playground on the site of the former Spooners mill dam and the paddling pools alongside the road, was created during the 1950s as part of the Festival of Britain. The original paddling pools used water flowing in from the River Rivelin – the inlets can be seen just above the weir below the café.

In 2013, the paddling pools were fully refurbished by Sheffield City Council, and reopened as 'Rivelin Valley Water Play'. The changes include a new toilet block, a new water filter system, improved access to the three large splash pads with anti-slip surfacing, a variety of water-play equipment, such as jets, sprinklers, bucket drops and water tables, and ramped access with handrails into the paddling pool. The improved facilities were partly funded by the 'Aiming High for Disabled Children' programme.

DID YOU KNOW? About 800,000 anvils were produced at Mousehole Forge during its working life, most of which were exported to the USA.

RIVELIN PARK CAFÉ TO GLEN BRIDGE

Distance: 1.3 km; 0.8 mile

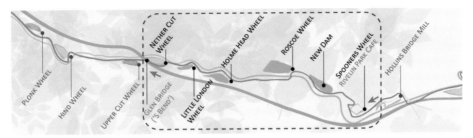

The café sits on the site of the next watermill, SPOONERS WHEEL [5]. **Follow the path past the café, alongside the play area** (built on the infilled **Spooners** mill dam (Fig. 25)) **and towards the concrete bridge over the river** (Fig. 26 shows the fore-runner of this bridge). **At this point, anyone wishing to avoid steps should cross the bridge and follow the river-side path to rejoin the trail at the next bridge (Roscoe Bridge). Otherwise, keep to the path up the slope by the slide and just before reaching the road (and before the Bridleway) turn left and go up five steps onto the footpath** (constructed by the Ranger service and the BTCV in 1997). **Follow the footpath and go down the steps to the overgrown NEW DAM [6], which lies in front of you.** At the bottom of the steps, the footpath crosses a small metal bridge over the overflow from **New Dam**. Look over the railing (on the mill dam side) and straight down to see grooves in the stones on either side of the channel at the deep drainage level – these are guides for the shuttle gate, which could be raised to drain the water out of the dam for maintenance. Just to the right of the overflow are the remains of the sluice that controlled the flow of water into the tunnel to **Spooners Wheel** mill dam.

Look at the photograph in Fig. 27 and try to imagine **New Dam** in the early twentieth century when it was used as a swimming pool! The water at that time would have been just below the level of the path along the dam wall, but the mill dam is now mainly dry, apart from a stream running through to the overflow, and there are some quite large Alder, Ash, Oak and Sycamore trees – all developed over the last 75 years or so. Look out for Celandine, Enchanter's Nightshade and Himalayan Balsam in the ground flora.

Follow the path along by the river. Between the path and the river is an extensive stand of an introduced garden species, Lesser Periwinkle, the blue flowers of which can be seen in spring and early summer. There is also a lot of Privet and Ground Elder here. Along this stretch of river bank (but best seen from the south side) are the remains of two foot bridges built in the early 20th century for better access to

Fig. 25. Spooners Wheel and mill dam (undated). The current café was built on the site of the workshops and the children's play area is on the infilled mill dam. St. Michael's Mortuary Chapel, Rivelin Glen Cemetery is behind, to the left. *Sheffield City Council, Libraries Archives and Information: www.picturesheffield.co.uk Image t01533.*

Fig. 26. The 'One Man Bridge' and ford/stepping stones near Spooners Wheel mill dam (*c.* 1900). The bridge (near the children's playground) has since been replaced. *From the KK collection.*

SPOONERS WHEEL (1630s–1930s)

Map reference: SK 3211 8836
Also known as: Holme Wheel, Rivelin Bridge Wheel, Rivelin Wheel, Spooners Wheels.
Main trades: Grinding files, saws, fenders, scythes and cutlery; knife forge.

Dating from at least 1637 (possibly before), **Spooners Wheel** was amongst the earliest to be built in the valley. The two mill houses, each with its own waterwheel located between the two buildings, stood where the Rivelin Park Café is today. The Websters of Cloughfields held a lease from at least 1637, but the first record of the Spooner family here is in 1716, when a lease names William Spooner and James Bromley. In 1794, a lease shows 16 trows, employing 24 men. Four fender trows, two saw trows, three file trows and five cutlers' trows were recorded in 1814.

The mill dam (Figs. 21 and 25) at **Spooners Wheel** was small and the amount of water retained was wholly inadequate to provide all the power needed, so the **New Dam** was constructed upstream in the early 1850s as a supplementary water supply.

In 1851, **Spooners Wheel** was sold by the Norfolk Estate to Thomas Blake, at which time there were 16 occupiers. Blake sold out to the Sheffield Waterworks Company only a few years later. In 1854 a new waterwheel on the north side was listed as 17 ft x 5 ft. In 1896 the south side was leased to Samuel Staniforth and in 1898 the north side to Joseph Simpson. By 1909 Samuel Staniforth owned the lease for both sides and reserved the right to convert the **New Dam** into public swimming baths (Fig. 27). The last person working at **Spooners Wheel** is thought to be a Mr Dawson (*c.* 1930) and the site was in ruins by 1936.

The mill dam was originally fed by a long head goit all the way from the weir (Figs. 1 and 28) above what is now the **New Dam**. Part of the goit was taken through a tunnel, which still exists, in the high ground between the **New Dam** and **Spooners Wheel** mill dam. A hole has opened up in the bank in the last few years which shows the location of this tunnel – this can be seen from the south side of the river. The children's playground was built on the site of the mill dam in the 1950s. No traces remain of the tail goit, which ran across what is now the grassed area in front of the café and straight into the **Hollins Bridge Mill** dam (Fig. 21).

Fig. 27. The changing sheds and swimming area of the New Dam, with allotments behind, in the early 20th century. New Dam was converted to a public swimming baths in 1909. *From the KK collection.*

Fig. 28. The New Dam weir (clearly overgrown) with Roscoe Wheel and cottages behind (undated). The shuttle mechanism on the inlet to the head goit, with roller and capstan, is mounted on the stones beside the girl. *Sheffield City Council, Libraries Archives and Information: www.picturesheffield.co.uk Image s10376.*

NEW DAM (1853–1930s)

Map reference: SK 3192 8835

Main uses: Extra water supply for **Spooners Wheel**, swimming pool.

As its name implies, the **New Dam** was the last mill dam in Rivelin to be constructed (possibly the last in Sheffield). It is the only one in the valley without an adjacent waterwheel. It was built in the early 1850s as a supplementary water supply for **Spooners Wheel** due to a demand for more water. The existing **Spooners** head goit was widened and water fed into the **Spooners** mill dam by means of an underground tunnel through the high bank between the two dams.

In 1909 Sheffield Council turned the **New Dam** into an open air swimming pool (Fig. 27) – this was for men and boys only, although this rule was apparently widely ignored! However, being set so low down in the valley the water was always cold and only the most hardy could stand it for more than a couple of minutes. The pool had a swimming attendant and a woollen costume could be rented from him for a penny. The pool also had quite a lot of fish in it – if you caught one of these fish and placed it in a bucket at the side of the office you would receive your penny back. The pool closed in the late 1930s when the long wooden shed that was used as changing facilities was destroyed by fire.

The mill dam was fed via a weir (Figs. 1 and 28) and very short head goit at the western end. The weir, now marked by the Rivelin Chair sculpture (page 38), is in poor condition. The drained mill dam is well-wooded, but has a stream flowing through. The overflow (at the eastern end) is now crossed by a bridge; water from the stream flows out of the dam at the deep drainage level and drops steeply into the river via a very short channel; the outlet from the dam into the **Spooner** tunnel is nearby.

the swimming pool. On the north bank of the river, two short lines of Privet bushes border a path from the edge of the remains of the eastern-most bridge. This marks the location of the turnstile for the swimming pool. By the 1970s, the bridges were in a poor state of repair and were removed.

Cross the entry to the head goit for New Dam, **marked by large stone blocks.** Hart's Tongue Fern can be seen in the walls of the head goit. **Walk up the slope a short distance** and look back to see grooves in the stonework for the wooden boards of the shuttle gate that used to control water flow into the head goit. At the river's edge here is a stand of Pendulous Sedge and a little further on Wood Melick and Yellow Archangel can be seen on the bank to the right of the path. **The RIVELIN CHAIR SCULPTURE (see below) sits on the remains of the New Dam weir.**

Continue on the path and walk down a few steps to cross the end of the tail goit from ROSCOE WHEEL [7]. Follow the footpath along the river to the early 19th century Grade II listed Roscoe Bridge (Fig. 6).

Before turning left to cross the bridge, take a look at the ruins of **Roscoe Wheel** and its mill dam, which lie just ahead of you to the right. There is a good example of a wheel pit here, where the size of the breast-shot waterwheel can be judged from the curved grooves in the walls. Water now drops into the wheel pit from the mill dam, runs across the floor and then into the tail goit, which is culverted underground at this point. Look towards the steps up the side of the bank – the square holes in the retaining wall supported the wooden beams for the first floor of the two-storey grinding hull that was built into the bank here. A stream runs through the large mill dam, now silted up and overgrown with trees including Alder, Beech, Sycamore and Willow.

Roscoe Wheel was linked to the hamlet at Clough Fields (Crosspool) via a cart track and the bridge, and to Stannington and Bradfield by the footpath that winds up the steps behind the Wheel into Roscoe Bank Plantation. This mature woodland is popular with squirrels as well as both resident woodland birds and summer migrants like Wood Warbler and Blackcap.

RIVELIN CHAIR SCULPTURE

The cast iron chair is crafted to appear like a seat made of coppice wood to reflect the thriving coppice industry that existed in the valley even before the watermills. It was designed and produced by local artist Jason Thomson who wanted to reflect other pieces of ironmongery around the valley left behind from the mills, and the twisted tree roots winding around the old dam walls. It was installed in June 2011, by Sheffield City Council.

Cross the river on Roscoe Bridge and turn right on the footpath (the river should now be to your right). [The footpath along the north bank leads to stepping stones, which may be impassable if the river is high.] The square hole in the stonework on the north river bank, and the massive stone blocks (with capstan and roller) on the dam wall behind, mark the overflow sluice from Roscoe mill dam. Further upstream, the top kerb of the weir at the inlet to this mill dam is unusual as it is formed of two arcs (Fig. 29) – to our knowledge the only one in Sheffield.

Benches were installed by the RVCG on both sides of the river here, the stepping stones reset and a small part of the wall by the river rebuilt. On the far (north) side of the river, immediately upstream from the Roscoe mill dam, is an area once used as a market garden. A German bomb fell here during the 'Sheffield Blitz' on 12th December 1940 – this is said to have blown out all the windows in the greenhouses on the nearby allotments!

Just beyond the stepping stones, on the left of the path, look up to see a tall tree stump on which is growing (about 6 feet up) a large bracket fungus – this has moss on the top and must be many years old. The edge-set stone slabs, joined by wrought-iron straps, that run along the edge of the river here are part of the tail goit from the next Wheel – the HOLME HEAD WHEEL [8]. As the wheel pit was lower than the river, this arrangement was needed to equalise the water levels and prevent water backing up the channel when river levels were high; a similar line of stonework can be seen at Hollins Bridge Mill and Third Coppice Wheel.

Continue on the path and down a slope towards Holme Head Wheel. On the river-bank at the bottom of the slope are some broken stone steps leading down to the

Fig. 29. The unusual Roscoe weir, with its double-arc top kerb and long slope.

ROSCOE WHEEL (c. 1725–1920s)

Map reference: SK 3171 8825
Also known as: Holme-Intack Wheel, Hoole's Wheel, Willow Bank Wheel.
Main trades: Cutlery, fender, file & saw grinding; polishing; blacking mill.

The **Roscoe Wheel** was 'newly erected' in 1725, with William Hoole & Joseph Spooner its earliest tenants. Records of 1794 show 12 trows and 16 men employed. It was engaged for the best part of its working life in the fender and saw grinding trade, for which huge grindstones, up to 7 ft in diameter, were required. In 1835, a valuation listed a blacking mill*, steam engine and boilers. The Wheel was unusual in the valley, having a breast-shot waterwheel and a two-storey building. The upper floor, reached via steps in the bank behind, housed a polishing shop – a process that used wooden wheels with a leather belt, coated in glue and powdered emery, running around them. In 1830, there seems to have been a second, smaller, building between the main building and the bridge, apparently driven by a second waterwheel.

A row of cottages under Roscoe Bank stood beside the Wheel (Figs. 1, 6 and 28). On the side of one of these cottages were painted the words "HOT WATER FOR TEAS" – this was supplied by the tenants to the many weekend picnickers escaping into the valley from the city, and no doubt provided a good source of extra income for them. Fig. 30 shows a photograph of the mill dam with buildings behind.

Roscoe Wheel was used until at least 1922 and recorded as derelict in 1936. Remains of the building can still be seen as well as the wheel pit arch and outfall from the pit into the tail goit (culverted underground). A curved groove in the wall of the wheel pit gives some idea of the size of the wheel.

The weir is still in good condition and is particularly unusual: the long, dressed stone slope has three changes of gradient, and there are two top kerbs –the upper one is a double-arc (Fig. 29), which is unique in Sheffield, apparently built to help protect the second kerb by causing silt to be deposited further upstream. Some iron-work survives on top of the large stone slabs of the head-goit entry. The short head goit now feeds into a stream that flows along the bottom of the hillslope at the edge of the now dry and wooded mill dam and to the river via the wheel pit/tail goit and the overflow. A capstan and roller are mounted on the massive stone blocks of the overflow (near Roscoe Bridge). The tail goit is culverted until about 50 m below the wheel pit, and then runs along the base of the hill slope and into the river close to the **New Dam** weir.

* a blacking mill ground charcoal into a fine powder used for the dusting of moulds in foundries and in the manufacture of lamp black and shoe polish.

river – these mark the location of stepping stones that used to cross the river here (Fig. 31). [These were replaced by the stepping stones downstream, put in when the path on the river bank opposite became eroded in the 1970s.] Take a few moments to look at the remains of the **Holme Head** wheel pit and workshop. In July 2009, the University of Sheffield Archaeology Department conducted a survey here and archaeology students excavated the small water-powered grinding workshop. The excavations revealed the concrete floor with grinding trows set into the floor, one of which contained a riveted metal frame and hooks for the chains which secured the wooden seat (known as a horsin) to the floor (see Fig. 4). Many broken knife blade blanks were found here.

The damp walls here provide an ideal habitat for ferns such as Hart's Tongue fern and liverworts such as the Great Scented Liverwort. Look out for the white flowers of Greater Stitchwort on the river bank here in spring. **Walk up the slope** to see on the left the large stones of the overflow – look out for the iron staples holding the top stones together, the low-level drain, slotted side stones and the remains of the roller mechanism for the shuttle gate. **Follow the path along the dam wall.** The river bank opposite is a good place to watch for Wrens (Fig. 39) darting about in the walls or undergrowth.

IN RIVELIN VALLEY Nº SHEFFIELD   G.B.&SONS.Nº 24

Fig. 30. Roscoe Wheel and mill dam (undated). *Sheffield City Council, Libraries Archives and Information: www.picturesheffield.co.uk Image y01883.*

The Holme Head mill dam is quite large but mostly overgrown, although still holding enough water to create a wetland habitat for amphibians and the more secretive birds like the Willow Tit. In 1934 the dam was reported to be nearly filled with Horsetails and as a result of further silting and drying it has now been largely succeeded by other vegetation including Brooklime, Forget-me-not, Great Hairy Willow Herb, Iris, Nettle, Reedmace (Bulrush) and some trees (mainly Alder and Willow). The rust-coloured stain at the upstream end of the dam is a result of water draining from the iron-rich mineral deposits in the Hagg Hill & Crosspool hillsides coming into contact with the air. The plants growing here include Creeping Buttercup, Horsetail, Opposite-leaved Golden Saxifrage, Soft Rush, Wavy Bitter-cress and Wood Sedge.

Cross the head goit beside the weir (Fig. 35). Rusted remains of the capstan & roller of the head goit shuttle mechanism can still be seen.

The footpath between Holme Head and Little London Wheel tends to be wet; drainage and re-surfacing work by the RVCG in 2013 aimed to alleviate this recurring problem. A brick-arched tunnel that linked the Little London tail goit to the Holme Head head goit was rediscovered whilst doing the drainage work here – only a few stones are now visible to the left of the path just above the weir. The large pipe outfall into the river just above the weir is a storm overflow pipe from the Crosspool area.

Fig. 31. Holme Head Wheel with stepping stones made of old grindstones, *c.* 1923. *Sheffield City Council, Libraries Archives and Information: www.picturesheffield.co.uk Image s10354.*

HOLME HEAD WHEEL (1740s–1930s)

Map reference: SK 3154 8803
Main trade: Grinding (mainly knives and razors).

The Holme Head Wheel was unusual in the valley as, together with Mousehole Forge, it did not originally belong to the Manor of Sheffield but to the Manor of Owlerton. The first record for this location is for a lease in 1742 to Nicholas Morton & William Shaw. It was subsequently taken over by Spooners and by 1794, Cadman & Co, razor makers, were running 11 trows and employing 15 men. The waterwheel was 11 ft diameter by 8 ft wide. By 1905 Holme Head was owned by Sheffield Waterworks Company, who let it to several tenants. It was disused but still in good condition in 1936. A painting of the interior (Fig. 4) gives an excellent insight into working conditions in the mid-19th century. Fig. 31 shows the buildings near the original stepping stones and Fig. 32 shows the mill dam with building behind in about 1931.

The steep, convex stone weir is deteriorating at the north end. Rusted remains of the capstan & roller of the head goit shuttle mechanism survive (the originals can be seen in Fig. 35). The tail goit from Little London Wheel, now blocked, used to run directly into the head goit of Holme Head alongside the weir. The mill dam is quite large and mostly overgrown, although still holds water. A few remains of the building, pentrough, wheel pit and the wheel spindle can still be seen. A roller survives on the overflow stonework; the water is culverted beneath the path and flows into the river through a small stone arch. The tail goit runs in a culvert beneath the path before emerging into the river just above the modern stepping stones, initially separated from the river by edge-set slabs joined by wrought-iron straps.

HOLME HEAD WHEEL

Fig. 32. Holme Head Wheel and mill dam c. 1931. Greenhouses can be seen to the left, on the opposite bank of the river.
Sheffield City Council, Libraries Archives and Information: www.picturesheffield.co.uk Image y00553.

LITTLE LONDON WHEEL (1752–1910s)

Map reference: SK 3135 8797
Main trades: Cutlery and file grinding.

Little London Wheel (Figs. 33–35) has one of the most straight-forward histories in the valley. In 1752 Robert Greaves leased part of the stream for 21 years with an annual rent of £1 and a liberty to erect a cutler's Wheel. In 1794 Thomas Spooner was running four trows and employing six men. The Wheel was in ruins by 1903 and was let for a nominal sum to Samuel Dawson (a file grinder) for him to repair. Dawson was evidently still there in 1905 (Fig. 33) but the Wheel was recorded as empty by 1907 and demolished in 1911. Some overgrown stonework is all that remains of the footings and wheel pit.

The mill dam was fed from the **Nether Cut** tail goit via a culvert, as well as from the river via a short head goit. The steep stone weir is in fair condition. There is a modern sluice gate on the head goit entry and remains of a staple can be seen on the lintel. The mill dam is now largely dry and well wooded, but a stream flows through to the overflow (located under the bridge carrying the path). The stonework of the overflow is well-preserved, with roller and capstan mounted on top and a low-level drain. The blocked tail goit is culverted towards **Holme Head**, but is now interrupted by the Crosspool storm pipe.

Mr Dawson outside the Little London Wheel

Fig. 33. Mr Dawson, tenant from *c*. 1903–1907, outside the Little London Wheel (*c*. 1905). *From the KK collection.*

Fig. 34. Drawing of Little London Wheel in the early 1900s, by Mr A. Chattle. *Courtesy of Mr M. Chattle.*

At this point the footpath forks: the right-hand path is rather uneven in places, so those wishing to keep to a level path should carry straight on, with LITTLE LONDON WHEEL [9] on your right, until you reach Nether Cut Wheel [10]. Otherwise, take the right-hand path and walk to a short, modern bridge. To the left, under the bridge, can be seen the well-preserved remains of the overflow from Little London mill dam. The low-level drainage point is now at the level of the stream, with slots in the stones on either side for the shuttle board – this was raised and lowered using the capstan/roller mechanism mounted on the stones above.

Cross the bridge and follow the path along the riverside on top of the Little London mill dam wall. The area on the left formerly occupied by the dam is now well wooded, mainly with Alder and Sycamore. A stream now flows through the dam; as at Holme Head, the rusty colour here is a result of water draining from iron-rich deposits in the hillside above. Great Woodrush can be seen in the mill dam. Cross the head goit beside the weir and continue towards the clearing at the foot of the NETHER CUT WHEEL [10]. The tail goit from Nether Cut is culverted beneath the path, emerging through a stone arch and running between the paths and straight into the Little London head goit just below the weir.

The Nether Cut mill dam was cleared and dredged in 1967, at which time it was stocked with Roach and Tench. It is still largely open water, now with trout and perch, and with a variety of wetland plant species such as

Fig. 35. Holme Head weir, with Little London Wheel behind (undated). Note the shuttle mechanism (left), with capstan and roller, on the head goit entry and the cow on the river bank (right). *Sheffield City Council, Libraries Archives and Information: www.picturesheffield.co.uk Image s10487.*

Fig. 36. Original oil painting of Nether Cut Wheel, 1857 (artist unknown).
Sheffield City Council, Libraries Archives and Information: www.picturesheffield.co.uk Image s22559.

Fig. 37. A rare view of the Nether Cut mill dam and Wheel taken from 'New Bridge' (now Glen Bridge) (*c.* 1910). The wall running across the right hand side of the photograph is alongside the 'New Road' (Rivelin Valley Road). *From the KK collection.*

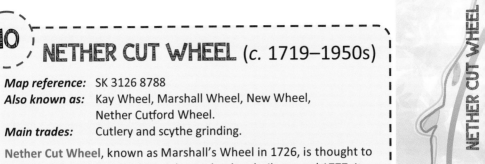

10 NETHER CUT WHEEL (c. 1719–1950s)

Map reference: SK 3126 8788
Also known as: Kay Wheel, Marshall Wheel, New Wheel, Nether Cutford Wheel.
Main trades: Cutlery and scythe grinding.

Nether Cut Wheel, known as Marshall's Wheel in 1726, is thought to have been built around 1719 and completely rebuilt around 1777. It originally ran four trows, but in 1794 had nine trows, employing 15 men. The mill suffered a rattening* incident in 1850 for using non-union labour – most of the mills in the valley used non-union labour but **Nether Cut** seems to have been singled out for special attention and was attacked on several occasions. The Sorby family leased the site for many years until 1920, when it moved into the hands of the Kay family who carried on grinding work for the Sorbys. Fig. 36 shows an artist's impression of the Wheel in the mid 19th century and Fig. 7 the derelict building, with pentrough and waterwheel, in 1954.

Nether Cut was the last mill in the valley to be worked by waterwheel; scythe grinding at one trow continued until at least 1939. The building was demolished as late as 1956 – all traces of it have been removed but the large mill dam has been preserved for fishing.

There was no weir, the mill dam being fed directly via the tail goit from **Upper Cut,** now running through a tunnel under the road (built in around 1906, see page 77). Water from the mill dam now outfalls into the river in two places: (1) mostly over an overflow and down a narrow stone channel and (2) culverted beneath the slope and into the tail goit, which runs between the two paths to feed directly into the **Little London** mill dam near the weir.

*Rattening: a series of attacks on 'blackleg' establishments by a militant faction among the emerging Trade Unions: collectively known as 'The Sheffield Outrages'. The attacks generally involved the removal of essential tools or items of equipment (often the driving bands of the grindstones) but in some cases escalated to arson and machine-breaking.

DID YOU KNOW? On Rivelin Valley Road near Glen Bridge are the remains of two quarries. Rivelin Grit stone was quarried from here and many more places in the valley, providing most if not all of the grindstones that were used here.

Angelica, Bitter-cress, Creeping Buttercup, Figwort, Horse-tail, Reedmace (Bulrush) and Water Mint. This is a popular spot for the Heron (Fig. 41) to fish and Grey Wagtails (Fig. 41) can often be seen on the exposed mud patches. In 2012, the RVCG undertook repairs to the stonework along the top of the dam wall near the overflow after some of the capping stones were stolen.

Walk up the track to join Rivelin Valley Road at Glen Bridge (known as the 'S Bend'), looking out for a patch of Wild Garlic on the bank to the left of the path.

Fig. 38. Upper Cut Wheel (foreground) at 'The Bridge' (Glen Bridge / S-bend) with Rivelin Glen behind (c. 1915). The line of swing-boats can be seen bottom left. *Sheffield City Council, Libraries Archives and Information: www.picturesheffield.co.uk Image y01884.*

Fig, 39. Dippers (left) are often seen along the river and goits. Wrens (right) are also regularly seen darting in and out of the old masonry. *Photographs: Andy Jones.*

48

GLEN BRIDGE TO WOLF WHEEL

Distance: 1.2 km; 0.7 mile

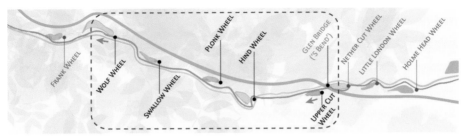

Note that the trail upstream of Glen Bridge is very uneven in places, with some steps and stepping stones.

At the top of the track from the Nether Cut mill dam, turn right for a short distance and cross the road at the bend, taking good care to watch for traffic. Take a moment to look over the railings at the remains of the UPPER CUT WHEEL [11] and its tail goit, then walk down the flight of steps at the 'Public Footpath' sign to re-join the riverside path.

The Upper Cut mill dam was very long and narrow, but the outline is now mostly obscured – partly by vegetation, but also partially infilled due to slippage from the hillside above. A stream now flows along the head goit and along the northern retaining wall of the mill dam. There is usually an attractive cascade of water from the dam into the wheel pit and the wall here provides an ideal damp habitat for ferns, mosses and liverworts, including the Great Scented Liverwort.

For about 200 metres the path runs along the bank between the head goit of Upper Cut Wheel and the river. A small bridge marks the entry to the head goit at the weir (Fig. 9). The tumbled-down walls on the opposite side of the river are a reminder of the old allotments, and stones along the edge of the river are the remains of an old trackway.

Continue along the path and cross the river at the next bridge, known as 'One Man Bridge' (Fig. 43). Beside the bridge is a ford where the bridleway crosses the river. There are now few traces of the HIND WHEEL [12] buildings, which stood near another of the RVCG cast iron mill markers (see right and page 26). **Follow the path up the slope and bear left onto the wall of Hind Wheel mill dam. Walk over the metal plates covering the overflow and follow the path around the water's edge.**

Mill marker at Hind Wheel.

Fig. 40. The Upper Cut Wheel with upturned boat (c. 1900). *Sheffield City Council, Libraries Archives and Information: www.picturesheffield.co.uk Image s10448.*

Fig. 41. Heron (above) and Grey Wagtail (left) are often seen along the river. Treecreepers (top left) search the bark for grubs. *Photographs Andy Jones.*

11 UPPER CUT WHEEL (c. 1749–1920s)

Map reference: SK 3117 8782
Also known as: New Wheel, Upper Cutford Wheel.
Main trades: Cutlery grinding, rowing boat hire, swing boats.

There is some confusion in the records between the **Upper Cut** and **Nether Cut** Wheels, but the first record for **Upper Cut** appears to be in a lease of 1749. In 1794 the wheel pit had a 13 ft 8 in fall of water; there were eight trows and 13 men employed. In 1818 it was rented by Bradshaw & Co for £7 per annum. Like **Nether Cut**, the Wheel was involved in a rattening case in 1874. Work ceased here around 1930.

The photographs in Figs. 38 and 40 show the mill dam and building in the early 20th century. **Upper Cut** used to be a hive of activity, not only at the Wheel, but also due to the many visitors who used to hire the rowing boats and enjoy rides on the swing boats located here (Fig. 38).

The low stone weir is deteriorating at the south-east end. There is a roller assembly (seen in Fig. 9) on the head goit lintel above a modern shuttle gate. A long head goit feeds water into the long and thin mill dam, now made even narrower due to slippage from the hillside above. Some of the better remains of a wheel pit in the valley exist here. Between the wheel pit and the river you can still make out the footings and walls of the mill buildings, partly obscured now under the path and steps up to Rivelin Valley Road. Water overflows directly from the dam into the wheel pit, from where the tail goit goes under the road and through a large stone archway into the **Nether Cut** mill dam. **Upper Cut** and **Nether Cut** were also linked via an overflow channel.

The **Hind Wheel** mill dam is one of the most popular in the valley and one on which the RVCG has done a lot of work. Have a picnic or just sit quietly and watch for Dippers (Fig. 39) or Heron (Fig. 41) feeding in the river above the ford or for a Treecreeper (Fig. 41) searching the bark for grubs. The mill dam is also a haven for dragonflies and at dusk one of the many popular feeding places for the large number of bats within the valley. Great Woodrush grows in abundance on the bank opposite the overflow.

The mill dam was dredged for fishing in 1967, at which time a Carp weighing over 30 lbs was rescued. It is still used for fishing, but after losing most of the fish in the 1990s when the shuttle gate gave way and the water drained out, it is mostly now stocked with small trout. As a result of the heavy storms in the winter of 2013–14, a hole formed in the

HIND WHEEL (1580s–1930s)

Map reference: SK 3088 8760
Also known as: Hyne Wheel, Iron Wheel. [The Round Dam.]
Main trades: Cutlery grinding; metal inserts for ladies corsets.

The Hind Wheel is the first to be recorded within the valley, in a rental of 1581. (To put this into historical perspective, Sir Francis Drake defeated the Spanish Armada just seven years later, in 1588). It was occupied by Thomas Hine, Robert Webster & John Swynden, paying a rent of £1 per year. In 1772 there were six trows, but by 1794 there were ten trows (powered by a 15 ft fall of water) and 12 men employed.

In the early 19th century, the site was occupied by Joseph Greaves & John Tillotson, who often fell out over the use of water. It soon became obvious that the dam was too small, so in the 1820s the workshops were rebuilt and the mill dam almost doubled in size to the 'round' shape that it still is today (Fig. 44). In 1830 two waterwheels were noted: the southern, 11 ft 6 in diameter x 5 ft wide, run by Greaves; the northern, 12 ft x 5 ft 6 in, run by Tillotson. Each waterwheel ran eight grinding trows.

Fig. 2 shows a view of the Rivelin valley with Hind Wheel building and mill dam in about 1900. One of the waterwheels was still working in the 1920s. Steel strip for ladies corsets was being made here before the site was abandoned in the 1930s. In the early 1950s, the waterwheels were still in place (Fig. 42) but all of the surrounding buildings had collapsed (Fig. 43 and Fig. 44). The ruins of the buildings were removed and the area landscaped.

The mill dam was built in what seems to be a natural meander in the river. The weir is interrupted by two islands with trees. A modern valve on the entry feeds water into the mill dam via a short head goit. Water from the mill dam (which is maintained for recreation) runs over a wide overflow, with a steep fall into the river. The tail goit is culverted under the track and joins the river just above the Upper Cut weir.

dam wall near to the overflow. This was quickly and expertly repaired by a member of the RVCG, thereby averting a collapse.

About half way round the mill dam a narrow stream, which originates higher up the hill on Bell Hagg, runs down the steep bank on the far side of the river. A Whitebeam has fallen across the river here – look for clusters of white flowers in spring and reddish fruits in autumn. The delta of silt forming at the inlet-end of the mill dam is overgrown with plants including Brooklime, Figwort, Forget-me-not, Great Hairy Willowherb and Iris, with Horsetails expanding into the open water.

Fig. 42. The two waterwheels at Hind Wheel, built in the 1820s, seen here in 1952. *Sheffield City Council, Libraries Archives and Information: www.picturesheffield.co.uk Image s10365.*

Fig. 43. Derelict Hind Wheel and footbridge, with Albion Terrace (Roscoe Bank) in background (undated, probably 1950s). *Sheffield City Council, Libraries Archives and Information: www.picturesheffield.co.uk Image s10362.*

In 2012, the invasive plant Floating Pennywort was found in the **Hind Wheel** mill dam. A native of North America, it was first found naturalised in Essex in 1990 (probably discarded from a garden pond), and is now rapidly increasing across the country as it is easily spread from small fragments. Left unchecked, this plant can completely choke waterways, and so attempts are being made to control its spread.

At the far end of the Hind Wheel mill dam, the path crosses the short head goit beside the weir. A Bird Cherry tree and Pink Purslane grow on the bank to the right of the path just past the weir. **About 50 metres further on, look up the bank to the right to see the remains of the PLONK WHEEL [13] and its mill dam.** This small dam was abandoned in the mid 19th century and is now barely recognisable. There are some quite mature trees, including Alder, Holly, Oak and Sycamore. Look out for Siskins and Greenfinches; in springtime this is a good place to find early summer migrants such as Blackcap and Wood Warbler.

Continue on the path, past the Plonk Wheel mill dam – the stream on the right of the path is all that is left of the tail goit from the **Swallow Wheel**, which fed directly into the **Plonk Wheel** head goit. On the far bank two moss-covered stone walls mark the position of an old track from Hagg Lane, which at one time crossed the river at a ford. **Just beyond the next clearing, the remains of the SWALLOW WHEEL [14] are set back on the right hand side behind the trees.**

In 1936 the **Swallow** mill dam was recorded as "empty and grass grown", but it was apparently reflooded by local anglers in the 1940s. In 2002, the RVCG cleared

SHF. 192.　　　THE ROUND POOL, RIVELIN VALLEY, SHEFFIELD.

Fig. 44. View of Hind Wheel mill dam ('The Round Pool') and derelict buildings (c. 1950). *From the KK collection.*

PLONK WHEEL (1737–1850s)

Map reference: SK 3075 8758
Also known as: Bobby Wheel, Sawbridge Mill (or Wheel), Siddall Wheel.
Main trades: Cutlery grinding, saw mill?

Joseph Swallow & Thomas Bower built **Plonk Wheel** in 1737 and by 1759 it was running four trows. In 1794 the wheel pit is recorded as having a fall of 13 ft 4 in, running five cutlers' trows, with eight men employed but by 1814 there were seven trows. In 1822 the tenant was Abraham Unwin, and there were two waterwheels. By 1852 property lists show the owner of the ruined Siddall Wheel as Maria Kirby who, after a dispute with the Sheffield Waterworks Company, accepted £550 for it in 1856. For some unknown reason the mill was never rebuilt or used again. One of the early names for the site tends to suggest that a saw-mill may have stood here.

Early 19th Century maps show that the tail goit from **Swallow Wheel** fed water directly into the first of two small **Plonk Wheel** mill dams, these latter being linked by a culvert through the hillside (Fig. 47). Some of the stones used in the 1960s for building the new path for the Nature Trail are said to have come from the **Plonk** weir, but it is not clear whether there was ever a weir here – there are some stone blocks set into the river by the north bank that could mark the remains, but a weir is not shown on old maps.

Having been abandoned over 150 years ago, and partly filled by slippage from the hillside above, the drained mill dam is in the final stages of silting up and is well wooded. Nothing remains of the mill building or tail goit, but parts of the head goit can still be seen in places as a channel between the path and the hillslope above.

vegetation at the upstream end of the dam and dug out three large ponds, after which water was re-introduced via a modern shuttle gate. The overflow was also dug out and the stonework rebuilt (see Fig. 46). Getting the water level just right was critical otherwise the path at the downstream end of the dam flooded. Grooves for washboards (used to raise the water level) can be seen in the stonework on either side of the overflow. The stonework on the path just below the dam was also re-built. A small grindstone found nearby in the river is set in the bank by the overflow (Fig. 45).

SWALLOW WHEEL (1690s–1900s)

Map reference: SK 3046 8752
Also known as: Lockwood Wheel.
Main trades: Cutlery and razor grinding.

Swallow Wheel dates from at least 1692, at which time Hugh Lockwood paid a rent of £1. It was occupied by Joseph Swallow (a cutler from Stannington) in 1699. In 1745 there were four trows. Nathan Dixon held the lease in trust for the Swallow children in 1766; by this time the rent had increased to £4 and the mill to five trows. There were further increases over the next few decades such that by 1794 records showed 13 trows employing 18 men and around 1814 there were ten cutlers' trows and four razor trows. The wheel pit had a fall of some 16 ft 4 in at this time and in 1858 the waterwheel was noted as being 12 ft in diameter by 7 ft 5 in wide. The Wheel was in ruins by 1905. The drawing in Fig. 48 shows the mill building in the late 19th century.

Water is deflected into the head goit by a curved weir built of large pitched stones, now in fairly poor condition. A modern shuttle gate controls water flow into the head goit. The main overflow was partially rebuilt in 2002 (Fig. 46). Another overflow, near the tail end of the mill dam, has a grill – this was built in the 1990s to help keep water moving through the mill dam. Water falls from this second overflow into a culvert under the path and into the river. Although now overgrown, the wheel pit and the line of the buildings can be made out; part of the stone floor is still in place and can be seen if not flooded.

The stone arch over the tail goit culvert (illustrated in Fig. 48) is in good repair. The long tail-goit originally joined the head goit of Plonk Wheel (Fig. 47), and parts can still be seen alongside the footpath, with water finding its way across the path into the river in places. Some stones from the tail goit were used to build the footpath.

The mill dam still holds water and is a wildlife haven. It is silted, partially overgrown and heavily shaded, with trees such as Alder and Willow growing in the water. There is a small patch of Reedmace (Bulrush) near the far bank. In spring, the white flowers of Wood Sorrel can be seen on the bank of the dam wall here, and Bluebells, Birch, Oak and Whitebeam grow on the slope above the dam opposite the overflow. Stand on the bank for a few minutes and see how many birds you can identify – this is one of the best places in the valley for seeing a Kingfisher (Fig. 10).

Continue on the river-side footpath. At the Swallow **weir cross two small bridges, the first over the** Swallow **head goit** (look out for the modern shuttle gate and iron staples linking the lintel stones) **and the second over the tail goit of the next site, the** Wolf Wheel**, where it runs into the river.** Bluebells grow on the bank to the right. High up on this steep bank, just before the footpath that climbs up to the road, there is a coal seam about 15 inches thick, but it is now obscured by vegetation. An important cross-valley route from Dore to Bradfield crossed the river here (Fig. 50). **Look out for the remains of the** WOLF WHEEL **[15] buildings to the right and then walk up the steps to the** Wolf **mill dam.**

Fig. 46. Members of the RVCG Task Team fixing the new gate to the overflow at Swallow Wheel in 2002. Note the size of the stones that were dug out and cut to re-build this overflow – a really heavy and smelly job.

Fig. 45 (opposite). Left: Speckled Wood butterfly. *Photograph Andy Jones.*
Right: Grindstone set into the bank at Swallow Wheel.

Fig. 47. Fairbank's map of Plonk and Swallow Wheels in 1814, showing the connection between them and the two mill dams at Plonk. *Sheffield City Council, Libraries Archives and Information: Sheffield Archives FC/P/SheD/486L.*

Fig. 48. Drawing of Swallow Wheel in about 1860, by Mr A. Chattle. The stone arch over the tail goit culvert is still in good repair and was reclaimed from the undergrowth by the RVCG in 2012. *Courtesy of Mr M. Chattle.*

DID YOU KNOW? The local name Hollin (as in Hollins Lane) refers to Holly, which is common in the Rivelin valley. Its leaves were cut as winter fodder for sheep and cattle from stands of trees known as hollins or holly haggs.

WOLF WHEEL TO RAILS ROAD

Distance: 1.3 km; 0.8 mile

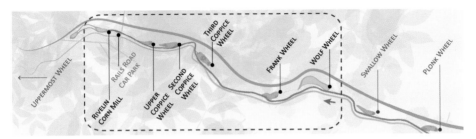

The **Wolf Wheel** mill dam (Fig. 49) is the largest in the valley still with open water. Overhanging oaks on the far bank provide wonderful autumn colours, with Goat Willow and Alder also at the water's edge. This is another great place to see nesting Mallard and Moorhens, and a Kingfisher (Fig. 10) can sometimes be seen perching on the fallen tree. Also look out for dragonflies, Great Diving Beetles, frogs and newts. By the 1960s it was becoming overgrown, but in 1967 the dam was dredged to restore open water, and stocked with Bream, Tench and Crucian Carp; it is still used for fishing. The unusual narrow stone bridge that takes the path over the overflow was also built in 1967, when the original Nature Trail was constructed.

The path follows the Wolf Wheel **mill dam wall, crossing the overflow and then the head goit close to the weir.** The tail goit from the next site upstream, FRANK WHEEL [16], can be seen on the right of the path. **With the bridge over the river to your left** (Fig. 51 shows a forerunner of this bridge)**, follow the path through the gap in the wall, marked by an old grindstone.** Walk along a short distance to see the supporting wall of the Frank Wheel mill dam, here without the usual protection of an earth embankment. Dog's Mercury and Ground Elder are abundant on the site of the former buildings. A stone monument at the bottom of the bank by the path commemorates the first ten years of the RVCG.

The Frank Wheel mill dam is heavily shaded by Alder, Beech, Hazel and Oak. As the overflow is close to the head goit entry, the water is mostly stagnant, giving a feeling of lifelessness. Some children call it the 'dinosaur pond' due to the fallen tree that sits halfway across the dam, with its branches in the water (Fig. 52). This gives the dam an eerie atmosphere especially on a cold frosty morning with the mist still hovering over the water. Sit a while and watch for birds – if you sit still enough and long enough you may well see a Kingfisher (Fig. 10).

Cross over the Frank **overflow** (now forming an attractive waterfall) **and up eight steps to follow the long head goit. Cross the head goit beside the weir** (where a Heron (Fig. 41) likes to sit). To the right there is an interesting patch of woodland

Fig. 49. Wolf Wheel mill dam, with buildings at the far end and River Rivelin below (to the right) (*c.* 1900). *From the KK collection.*

Fig. 50. The grinding room at Wolf Wheel, probably the largest in the valley (undated). The footbridge marks the cross-valley route from Dore to Bradfield, which climbs the steep bank behind the building. Note also the cultivated land on the slopes nearby. *From the KK collection.*

WOLF WHEEL (1720s–1930s)

Map reference: SK 3018 8750
Also known as: Rocher Wheel, Rocker Wheel.
Main trades: Cutlery and razor grinding.

Wolf Wheel was built in the early 1720s. In 1794, there were 11 trows with 16 men employed. By 1830 an iron overshot waterwheel (15 ft x 6 ft 8 in) ran 17 table-knife trows and two razor trows, making it probably the largest grinding room in the valley. James & Samuel Windle rented the mill from 1810–1852. In 1838 the Windles were in such disagreement over their business affairs that arbitrators were called in. Samuel subsequently sold his half of the mill to Joseph, who in 1852 sold the Wheel to the Sheffield Waterworks Company. Wolf Wheel was last recorded as being used in 1930, but the pentrough and shuttles were reported in good working order in 1934. Fig. 49 shows the mill dam, with the buildings just visible behind and Fig. 50 provides a good view of the large grinding room.

The four-bay weir is in good condition. The shuttle on the head goit entry has been replaced by a modern gate. The mill dam is the largest in the valley maintained for recreational use. The stone bridge that crosses the overflow was built in 1967 and in 2005 Sheffield City Council reinforced the dam wall alongside the river, to help prevent erosion and potential collapse. The wheel pit is partly infilled and overgrown but some remains of the buildings can still be seen. The long tail-goit runs into the river just above the Swallow weir.

where some large Beeches are mixed with Oak and Sycamore, as well as a few tall pine trees. Look out for Bluebells and the attractive grass Wood Melick. **Continue to the large grassy area ahead**, with two large oaks in the middle, which is a good place to look for butterflies on a sunny day and bats on a summer evening; Blackbirds and Song Thrushes may be seen feeding and the Robin's song heard, particularly in autumn and winter when other birds are quiet. This area is managed as part of a covenant agreement set up in around 1915 when Sheffield City Council acquired the land from the Norfolk Estate and **King Edward VII hospital** was built (see page 67).

As you **cross the clearing**, look down at the river to see a low stone wall (covered in moss and Great Woodrush), which marks the end of the tail goit from **Third Coppice Wheel**. **Enter the woodland and keep left along the indistinct, narrow path that follows the river bank.** A few metres along the path look across to the waterfall on the Black Brook – this is one of the few streams that drain into the valley. Clean water from here was fed into the **Third Coppice Wheel** (Rivelin Paper Mill) via an aqueduct across the river. This is another good place from which to watch for birds.

Continue on the path and cross the tail goit where it goes under the path towards the river, and go up the steps to THIRD COPPICE WHEEL **[17].** Water was re-introduced here by the RVCG in 2001 (with help from the Sheffield Conservation Volunteers), by re-building the collapsed overflow, topping with a new series of stepping-stones (Fig. 54) and fitting a new shuttle gate on the head goit entry. In 1936 there were many Irises in the mill dam, but these have disappeared and it is now heavily shaded by Alder, Sycamore and Willow. Plants seen around this dam include Creeping Buttercup, Goose-grass, Nettle, Golden Saxifrage, Pendulous Sedge, Stitchwort and Water Mint.

Cross the Third Coppice **overflow on the stepping stones to reach the large weir/ waterfall to your left** – one of the most attractive in the valley (Fig. 55). Look out for the large metal straps holding the stone blocks together along the top. Across the river from the weir there is a different type of woodland from that which edges

FRANK WHEEL, RIVELIN.

Fig. 51. Drawing of Frank Wheel in about 1850, by Mr A. Chattle. There is still a footbridge in this location. *Courtesy of Mr M. Chattle.*

16 — FRANK WHEEL (1730s–1900s)

Map reference: SK 2996 8736
Also known as: Coppey Nook, Coppy Wheel, Fourth Coppey Wheel, Frank Paper Mill, Nether Coppice Wheel.
Main trades: Cutlery grinding; paper mill.

The first lease for **Frank Wheel** was in 1737, to Richard Marshall and Stephen Parker. Marshall extended it in 1756 and in 1782 it was recorded as having 11 trows, employing 14 men, and an 18 ft 10 in fall of water. In 1852 the Wheel was still being used for cutlery grinding, but by 1854 it had been converted to a paper mill. The drawing in Fig. 51 shows what the building was like in the mid-19th century.

The last known lease on the Wheel, for 14 years, was recorded in 1889 between Sheffield Corporation and Horatio & Thomas Marsden. It stood empty by 1905 and most of the building was levelled. Part of the west end of the wheel building and part of a substantial wall that formed support for the pentrough can still be seen.

The weir of uncut stones is in fairly good condition, deflecting water through a small inlet and into a long, wide head goit. The wide overflow is situated at the west (head) end of the mill dam; grooves for washboards (used to raise the water level) can be seen in the stonework on either side. The overflow level was adjusted by the RVCG to allow more water to fill the dam (a delicate operation that took some time to get right because if it is raised too much the dam leaks). The tail goit is culverted beneath the track to the east, and runs directly into the head goit of the **Wolf Wheel** mill dam.

Fig. 52.
The 'dinosaur' tree at Frank Wheel mill dam.

Fig. 53. Third Coppice Wheel (Rivelin Paper Mill) with its associated buildings and distinctive tall chimney (1876). *Sheffield City Council, Libraries Archives and Information: www.picturesheffield.co.uk Image s10466.*

Fig. 54. In 2001, RVCG Task Team members re-built the collapsed overflow at Third Coppice and set a new row of stepping stones. Getting the height just right so that water passes through the stones but not over them was critical.

17 THIRD COPPICE WHEEL (1750s–1900s)

Map reference: SK 2954 8735
Also known as: Rivelin Paper Mill.
Main trades: Cutlery grinding; paper mill; rolling house.

The first lease for **Third Coppice Wheel** was in 1758 to John Hoyland & Joseph Spooner for 21 years. By 1794, the lease had passed to William Creswick who employed four men at four cutlers' trows, but by 1814, when it was converted to a paper mill, there were 13 trows. Paper-making (from rags) at this mill required good clean water, which was brought across from the Black Brook (on the opposite side of the river) in an aqueduct from just above the waterfall. It is hard to believe that there was once an extensive complex of buildings here, as the site is now largely obscured by landslip, but in 1852 the property comprised one paper mill, two drying houses, a rope shed, a long rolling house, stables and cowshed, and a dwelling, along with several other buildings. The photograph in Fig. 53 shows the site in the second half of the 19th century, at which time there was a tall chimney. Like **Frank Wheel** (next downstream), the last known lease for this property was to Horatio & Thomas Marsden in 1889. By 1905 both sites were described as empty.

The weir uses a natural waterfall raised by a single course of stone blocks stapled together (Fig. 55). The head goit is very short, now with a modern shuttle gate on the entry. The mill dam still holds water, but is silted and partially overgrown. The overflow (now crossed by stepping stones built by the RVCG in 2001, Fig. 54) is only a few metres from the head goit entry.

The bottom of the wheel pit was below the level of the river in order to increase the fall of water, thereby allowing a larger waterwheel to be used – in 1794 the wheel pit was recorded as having a fall of 18 ft 4 in. The long tail-goit (*c.* 150 m), which in the lower part is separated from the river by a low stone wall (now broken in places), allowed the fall in the river to match the water level in the tail goit and avoid water backing up the channel.

DID YOU KNOW? Samuel Fox, who leased **Upper Coppice Wheel** in the mid-19th century, established a wire-drawing business at a mill in Stocksbridge (just north of Sheffield) that developed into a steelworks, which became the major steel manufacturing complex of today.

much of the river. The trees are mainly oak but in the middle are some large Beeches. Beech casts a very heavy shade and has its main roots just below the surface, so that the undergrowth is sparse except for a few fungi in autumn. Here Blue Tit, Great Tit, Long-tailed Tit (Fig. 10) and Coal Tit may be seen, in pairs in summer or in larger mixed flocks in winter, with Goldcrest and Treecreeper (Fig. 41). This part of the river is also a good place to watch for Dippers (Fig. 39), particularly in spring and summer. These birds are rarely seen far from water; they perch on stones in the stream and bob up and down ('dipping') while feeding on small insects.

There are two trail options here, depending on river conditions:

(A) The main trail continues up the steps and around the top of the cliff. Look across Rivelin Valley Road to see the top of the main building of the former **King Edward VII Hospital** (see page 67). **Where the path forks, keep left and go down the path to** SECOND COPPICE WHEEL [18].

(B) For the more adventurous, when the river level is low, the SECOND COPPICE WHEEL [18] **can be reached by carefully crossing the river on the weir, walking a short distance along the bank and then back across the river via the stepping stones.** At the side of the river by the stepping stones, there is a steep cliff with water running down it – the water is sometimes rusty-coloured from the iron in the rocks. The cliff (known as 'Cryptogam Cliff') is made up of softer shales between beds of harder sandstone – water can pass through the porous sandstone but not

Fig. 55. Weir and waterfall at Third Coppice Wheel (*c.* 1950). *From the KK collection.*

KING EDWARD VII HOSPITAL

After King Edward VII died in 1910, the people of Sheffield donated £18,000 towards a memorial and it was decided to build a hospital for disabled children with the funds. The City Council provided extra cash and the Duke of Norfolk donated the land for the new hospital. The hospital, comprising 120–130 beds together with an operating theatre, kitchens and nurses quarters, received its first patients in 1916. The Hospital was known as the King Edward VII Hospital for Crippled Children, as reflected on an early map of the site (Fig. 56). Initially the patients were children with tubercular joints and rickets but as the years passed the type of condition treated was extended to include congenital deformities and poliomyelitis. From 1922 patients were also admitted from outside Sheffield. In 1939 it was decided to admit adult patients suffering from surgical tuberculosis.

In 1944, towards the end of the Second World War, beds were made available for wounded officers and both children and the officers seemed to benefit from each other's company. Also in that year the Hospital was recognised as a nurses' training hospital. In 1948, following the establishment of the National Health Service, the Hospital was renamed the King Edward VII Orthopaedic Hospital and additional facilities were introduced, including two new ward blocks, bedrooms for members of staff, and a workshop. A hydrotherapy pool was added in 1956. By then the hospital compared favourably with almost any in the Country.

The Hospital was closed in 1992 and converted for residential use after planning permission was granted in 1997. The hospital building, the entrance lodge, boiler house and one of the outbuildings are all Grade II listed.

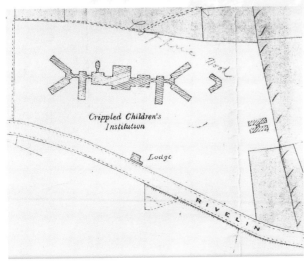

Crippled Children's Institution

Lodge

RIVELIN

Fig. 56. Extract from early 20th century map showing the "Crippled Children's Institution" (King Edward VII Hospital) on Rivelin Valley Road.

18 SECOND COPPICE WHEEL (1730s–1900s)

Map reference: SK 2942 8735
Also known as: Darwin Wheel, Middle Coppice, Rivelin Mill.
Main trades: Knife, scythe and saw grinding, wire-drawing mill, shops.

Built in 1736 by Joshua Spooner, a 'respected grinder', the Spooner family held the lease at **Second Coppice Wheel** until 1783. In 1794 it was being run by Benjamin Barker who employed three men working at three trows, the wheel pit at this time having a fall of 15 ft 4 in.

The Wheel became known locally as the Darwin Wheel after a widow named Darwin became a tenant in 1815, at which time scythes and saws were ground here. By 1852 the site included a grinding hull, a wire-drawing mill, shops and dwellings. In 1870 it was run by Joel Horsfield, who paid £95 per year for the tenancy of **Second** and **Upper Coppice Wheels**, but he subsequently abandoned the tenancy of **Second Coppice** because it was deemed unsafe. Estimates for the repairs came to £88 in 1871 and £125 in 1872. The works managed to keep going until at least 1905, at which time they were occupied by Greaves brothers & Hawley.

There is no weir at **Second Coppice** – water feeds into the head goit directly from the tail goit and overflow of **Upper Coppice**. The earth bank retaining wall is still in a fair condition and holds water but the mill dam is now very silted. In 2002, a new sluice gate was fitted on the overflow, which is at the head of the mill dam; water from the overflow travels under the path and into the river. Some overgrown walls of the buildings are still evident. The short tail goit can easily be traced to the river by the large retaining wall; this emerges just above the weir of the **Third Coppice**, by the stepping stones under 'Cryptogam Cliff'.

the shale, so water is forced to run down the cliff-face. This makes ideal wet conditions for ferns (such as the Lady Fern and Hard Fern), mosses and liverworts, as well as Great Woodrush. The small flowering plant on the cliff with tiny yellow flowers from March to May is Golden Saxifrage.

The RVCG undertook a lot of work on the **Second Coppice** mill dam in 2002. Then completely dry and overgrown, water was re-introduced by fitting a new sluice gate on the overflow to raise its level. A machine was used to dig a ditch along the edge of the dam to provide a channel for the water. Work still needs to be done to provide an outflow at the downstream end of the dam so that water can move through. Raising the water level killed many of the trees, but the dam is still quite shaded by Alder and Sycamore and a large Beech tree on the northern side. Plants growing in the water include Marsh Marigold and Water Mint. Dog's Mercury and Celandine are abundant on the dam wall.

Birds recorded in this area include Blue Tit, Coal Tit, Long-tailed Tit (Fig. 10), Goldcrest, Great spotted Woodpecker, Nuthatch and Treecreeper (Fig. 41).

Continue on the river-side path to find the third of the cast-iron mill markers (see below and page 26), **installed in 2007 near the wheel pit of** UPPER COPPICE WHEEL [19]. Just downstream from here is the deep pool used for years by local youths for jumping into the river and swimming. Here something of the geology of the area can be seen. The thick beds of resistant sandstone like the one forming the waterfall (Heyden Rock) alternate with softer shales which are easily eroded and in which the deep pool is formed.

The small **Upper Coppice** mill dam is silted, overgrown and well shaded, but there is a distinct stream flowing through it. In 2002 the RVCG introduced a small amount of open water to the dam by digging a pond in the centre and cleaning out around the overflow. The overflow itself was also raised and bricked up to divert the water across to the wheel pit. This raised the water level by around four inches but the mud has since slid forward and nearly filled the dam again.

The path follows the mill dam wall and then the bank between the head goit and the river, crossing the start of the head goit beside the weir just below the Packhorse Bridge (Fig. 57). This Grade II listed bridge, which is only about 1 m wide and with walls 60 cm high, dates from about 1775

and carried the packhorse track from Crosspool to Stannington. Look for the iron clamps holding the stones along the top together.

The end of the tunnel that used to carry the water from the **Rivelin Corn Mill** tail goit into the **Upper Coppice** head goit can be seen to the right of the path here. The weir is in poor condition although it still retains enough water in the river to cast a wonderful reflection of the bridge.

You are nearly at the end of the trail, so pause a while; stand in the middle of the bridge, look down-stream and try to imagine how different the valley must have looked in its different phases since the waters of the river were first used in the Middle Ages to provide water-power. Many of the trees of the valley can be seen

Marker at Upper Coppice Wheel.

Fig. 57. Packhorse Bridge (at Rails Road), dates from before 1790 and carried the track from Crosspool to Stannington. This photograph is undated (probably late 19th century), but the weir was clearly in quite an overgrown state at this time. *From the KK collection.*

Fig. 58. Corn grinding floor at Rivelin Corn Mill, with two sets of millstones (1948). The corn was fed onto the stones from the loading bay on the floor above. *Sheffield City Council, Libraries Archives and Information: www.picturesheffield.co.uk Image s09622.*

19 UPPER COPPICE WHEEL (1730s–1900s)

Map reference: SK 2930 8728
Main trades: Cutlery grinding, wire drawing.

Upper Coppice Wheel was built in 1736 by George Ibbotson after he had leased the land from the Duke of Norfolk for 21 years. The next recorded lease was to Thomas Spooner in 1761 and the mill stayed in the hands of the Spooner Family for the next 33 years. In 1794 the wheel pit was recorded as having a 12 ft fall of water, running four trows with six people employed.

There was extensive renovation work, including a new waterwheel, in the early 19th century. The Duke of Norfolk Estates remained the owners until 1854 when Sheffield Waterworks Company acquired all of the Coppice Wheels, and at which time the **Upper Coppice** was leased as a wire mill to Samuel Fox & William Rose. The mill was out of use by 1905.

The block-stone weir is in poor condition. The short head goit is culverted under the path by the weir and joined here by the tail goit from **Rivelin Corn Mill**. The small mill dam is silted and overgrown, with a stream flowing through. Few traces of the buildings remain, and the fall of water at the wheel pit has reduced from 12 ft to around 5 ft due to infilling with debris. The small overflow is alongside the wheel pit and the stonework of both is still in a fair condition. The water from the overflow now joins the water flowing into the wheel pit and runs directly into the head goit of the **Second Coppice Wheel**. At one time the overflow and tail goit would have run separately, with the water from the overflow running into a culvert under the path and flowing into the head goit lower down – this culvert can still be seen.

around the mill dam and near the bridge, including Ash, Alder, Beech, Elm, Elder, Hawthorn, Holly, Oak, Rowan, Sycamore and Willow.

To the right of the bridge, follow the path up a few steps to cross a grassy area, from where four steps lead directly onto Rails Road – take care when crossing the road at this point. Almost opposite is the car park that now occupies the site of the RIVELIN CORN MILL [20].

The corn mill and its mill dam were built around 400 years ago. The map in Fig. 59 shows the location of the mill buildings and houses that stood here until 1950, of which few traces now remain. Standing at what is now the junction of Manchester Road and Rivelin Valley Road and near

RIVELIN CORN MILL (c. 1600s–1950s)

Map reference: SK 2910 8725
Also known as: Rivelin Mills
Main trade: Corn mill.

The Rivelin Corn Mill and a hamlet of houses (Fig. 59) stood on the site of the Rails Road car park. The mill was always used for the grinding of corn and is believed to date back to around 1600 (making it one of the earliest in the valley), at which time it was owned by the Earl of Shrewsbury. The first clear reference to it shows Robert Rawson, John Swift & Edward Adamson as the tenants in 1632. In 1711 a lease was taken for 21 years by four men, all from Bradfield: James Crapper, William Ibbotson, Rowland Revill and Edward Barber. The lease was underwritten by 44 inhabitants of Bradfield who were responsible for the rent should the millers not fulfil their commitments.

By 1830 the mill was prospering and running two overshot waterwheels, one 15 ft x 4 ft and the other 14 ft x 4 ft, each wheel driving three pairs of millstones. However, in the summer months, shortages of water meant that out of the six pairs of stones only one set could be run for up to four hours per day. Following the building of the Rivelin Dams upstream in the 1840s, after which the water supply improved, the mill was sold to Sheffield Waterworks Company in 1856. It remained working until the mid-1920s and was still in working order in 1934, although in a poor state of repair by 1939; it was demolished around 1950. The photograph in Fig. 60 shows one of the dwellings. Fig. 58 shows two sets of millstones in around 1948, just before demolition.

The mill dam is fed through the head goit from a weir about 300 m upstream (on the south side of the A57 Manchester Road); the head goit was bridged by the 'Glossop Turnpike' in 1824. The long, narrow mill dam was reconfigured in 2006–2007, leaving two ponds linked by a culvert through the infilled section, but the re-built overflow remains in its original position. The tail goit runs under Rails Road directly into the Upper Coppice head goit near to the weir.

Fig. 59. Map showing the extent of the buildings at Rivelin Corn Mill in 1864.
Sheffield City Council, Libraries Archives and Information: Sheffield Archives SP56/1/2.

Marker at Rivelin Corn Mill.

the former Rivelin Post Office and café, this was, and still remains, a regular stopping-off point for walkers and travellers.

The fourth of the RVCG cast-iron mill markers stands here, this one depicting an ear of corn (see left and page 26).

Strengthening of the Rivelin Corn Mill dam wall took place in 1967, obscuring most of the outlines of the ruined buildings that stood along the overgrown north bank of the river (between the car park and the overflow). However, the dam wall developed a leak due to dredging activity around this time – this was meant to remove excess sludge and weeds but also removed some of the waterproofing clay lining from around the edge. The wall eventually collapsed during the winter of 2001–2 and the water from the dam poured out into the river below. The increasingly overgrown mill dam remained empty for about five years

Fig. 60. Dwelling at Rivelin Corn Mill (undated, probably early 1900s).
From the KK collection.

until, because of its importance and strategic location, the RVCG started a campaign, headed by its then chairman, Roger Kite, to have the dam fully restored. The estimated cost of £400,000 was too high for Sheffield City Council to fund, so other designs and funding were sought, and plans for infilling part of the dam were finally agreed in 2006. SCC and RVCG undertook an ambitious project in 2006–7 to rejuvenate the area by reducing the size of the dam by two-thirds, rebuilding the inner walls and creating a wildflower meadow and ground-nesting bird 'refuge' area. The bird feeding station here attracts Pheasant, Mallard and Moorhen in addition to the more usual bird-table species. The RVCG has also built a pond-dipping platform (Fig. 61) in the area of the old corn mill forebay, a picnic and barbecue area, additional seating and an outdoor classroom. The official opening was on 17th May 2007, celebrating a wonderful monument to those who established the mill over 400 years ago and a beautiful area to be enjoyed by visitors today.

The main part of the trail ends here as the UPPERMOST WHEEL [21] is on private land and not normally accessible. However, there are two more features of interest just past the Rails Road car park, which can be seen by following the path a short distance upstream. The 50 m (165 ft) long willow tunnel, was planted in 2010 in the grassy area between the two parts of the mill dam, using around 1000 willow whips to create what may well be the longest willow tunnel in Britain. More willow trees were planted in this area in 2014. Beyond the willow tunnel, the stone bridge that spans the river dates from 1819 and is Grade II listed. It was built to carry the Sheffield to Glossop turnpike road (which followed what is now the A57-Snake Pass route) across the river as well as across the **Rivelin Corn Mill** head goit.

Fig. 61. Pond-dipping platform at Rivelin Corn Mill (Rails Road).

UPPERMOST WHEEL (1750s–1840s)

Map reference: *c.* SK 2871 8687
Main trade: Cutlery grinding.

Uppermost Wheel was described in 1751 as newly built, and had four trows; Edward Nicholls was the Lessee with a 21 year tenancy. The rebuilding of 1772 and an increase in the rent from £1 0s 0d to £1 11s 6d suggest that extra buildings were added. In 1794, the tenant was William Greaves; the wheel pit had a fall of some 15 ft but only ran three trows. George Woollen, who also rented the Rivelin Corn Mill (next downstream), paid the rent from about 1799 up to 1845, by which time the Wheel had been pulled down.

Uppermost Wheel was situated near to the current water treatment works (Yorkshire Water), about 400 m upstream of Rivelin Corn Mill, (Fig. 62). Sheffield Waterworks Company built a 'depositing pond' (reservoir) across the river in this location in about 1869 to both smooth out compensation flows and to allow some of the suspended sediment to settle out before the water was released into the Rivelin. However, the remains of Uppermost weir, mill dam and Wheel appear to have been obliterated before this time as they are not shown on the first edition 6" Ordnance Survey map (surveyed in 1850–51). The site is now on private land and is not normally accessible.

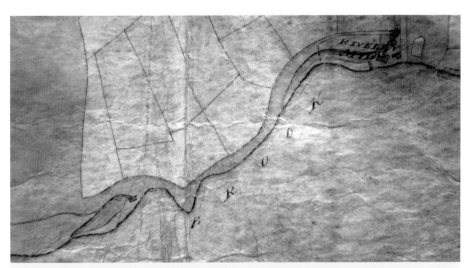

Fig. 62. Extract from Sheffield Enclosure Award map (1805) showing location of Uppermost Wheel (bottom left – unnamed) and Rivelin Corn Mill (top right). *Sheffield City Council, Libraries Archives and Information: Sheffield Archives ACM/S/70: ACM (Arundel Castle Manuscripts) reproduced with permission from His Grace the Duke of Norfolk, DL and the Director of Culture, Sheffield City Council.*

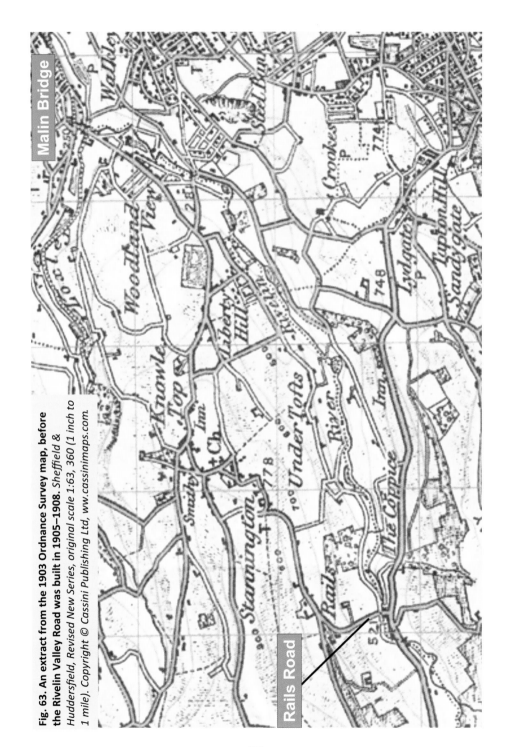

Fig. 63. An extract from the 1903 Ordnance Survey map, before the Rivelin Valley Road was built in 1905–1908. *Sheffield & Huddersfield, Revised New Series, original scale 1:63, 360 (1 inch to 1 mile). Copyright © Cassini Publishing Ltd, ww.cassinimaps.com.*

Rivelin Valley Road

Until the beginning of the 20th century, there was no through-route along the valley-bottom between Malin Bridge and Rails Road (Fig. 63). Links across the valley were by a series of paths, bridle-roads and cart tracks that connected the watermills with nearby settlements and Sheffield. Talk of a road through the lower Rivelin valley was ongoing for quite a few years, and in 1905 the decision was made to build it, seemingly influenced by the huge unemployment of the time. Most of the land was already owned by the Sheffield Corporation, although it was also necessary to buy some land from private owners. At around the same time the Corporation also bought some land in the valley for use as allotments (again, in order to assist the unemployed), and the Duke of Norfolk gave additional land between the road and the river for recreational purposes.

Work was started in November 1905 and originally provided full-time employment for 172 men. However, after intervention by the Sheffield Council Distress Committee in 1906, it was recommended that the workers should only work a three-day week to help provide employment for more men. It was subsequently decided that they should instead work alternate weeks. The average wage for these workers was about 10 shillings a week for a labourer and around 38 shillings for masons and pavers. The road cost around £30,000 to construct and was quickly nicknamed the 'New Road' by the locals. Work on the New Road was completed in June 1908 and, due to the success by the council of employing so many men from the Distress Lists, plans were drawn up to provide better access to the New Road from Walkley and Crookes.

In 1906, 700 lime trees were bought from Dixon's of Chester for £147. These were planted along both sides of the road for about 3 miles, one of the longest corridors of such trees in the country, and a delight of colour all year round. To protect the trees from vandals (yes they had them then as well!) they were each given a protective steel cage about 40 cm in diameter and 1.5 m tall. These cages were in place for at least 25 years. The newly-built road and young trees can be seen in Figs. 12, 37 and 38.

The Rivelin valley was well known for its wooded areas and had some of the largest trees in the city. To save money on construction, instead of being felled, some of these larger trees were left in place and protruded out into the new road. The trunks of these trees were painted white to warn oncoming motorists of the danger. It wasn't until a few years later, with the introduction of a 30 mph speed limit and quite a few fatalities, that these trees were removed.

RIVELIN VALLEY CONSERVATION GROUP

Working to promote the protection and the management of the Rivelin valley and its wildlife.

The Rivelin Valley Conservation Group was set up in 1991 and now has a membership of over 500, drawn mostly from the surrounding neighbourhoods, but with a substantial number city-wide and even beyond. The group acts in a wide variety of ways to help maintain public access and to promote the protection and management of Rivelin's countryside, wildlife and historical interest. Monthly evening meetings, with a speaker, give an opportunity to meet others and discuss valley matters. Amongst other activities, a Task Team meets in the valley once a month to work on a variety of practical management tasks.

The RVCG is completely independent, has its own constitution and is managed by an annually-elected executive committee. The group won the Sheffield Telegraph Environment Award (Community Trophy) in 2009 and 2011.

For more details and a membership form, please visit the RVCG website:

www.rivelinvalley.org.uk

Please remember, when visiting the Rivelin valley:

**For the enjoyment of others
Leave nothing but footprints
Take nothing but photographs
Kill nothing but time**

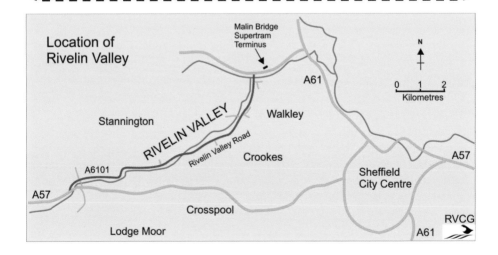

Location of Rivelin Valley

Planning and development in the Rivelin valley

A provisional Green Belt to protect the countryside around Sheffield, including the open land within the Rivelin valley, was introduced by Sheffield County Borough Council in 1938. At that time the Green Belt had no statutory weight, but the Council also purchased land west of the city's built-up area to ensure that it remained open and was not developed. Through the 1960s and 1970s, the Green Belt was gradually extended to create a buffer zone around the city and in 1983 the Green Belt within the city boundary was officially adopted by Sheffield City Council. Currently, and for the foreseeable future, the Sheffield Green Belt covers all the open land within the Rivelin valley, extending westwards to the boundary of the Peak District National Park.

Since the Green Belt was approved, new residential development has largely been prevented, despite increasing pressure, and the open character of the Rivelin valley, which comprises one of the most attractive landscapes in the City, has generally been protected, and, with the help of the Rivelin Valley Conservation Group, enhanced. Government and City planning policies have allowed a limited range of developments in the Green Belt, such as new agricultural buildings, small-scale stables and the alteration and conversion of farmhouses and agricultural buildings to residential and other uses. Within the terms of these policies many planning applications have been successful.

Most of the dwelling proposals have been on the northern side of the valley. To the south, between the A57 and the river, the main changes, following the sale of land by the City Council, have reflected the increasing demand for stabling and grazing horses. From a town planning perspective, this is a relatively unregulated activity about which the RVCG has been concerned for many years. The RVCG recognises that the use of land in the valley is changing as the nature of agriculture changes and other activities increase in popularity. However, whilst accepting that change is inevitable, the RVCG has always sought, through its comments and advice to the City Council on planning proposals, to ensure that any developments which do proceed fully reflect the character, amenity and landscape quality of the Rivelin valley.

RVCG Planning Team

FAIRWELL TO RIVELIN
Extract from a poem by Ebenezer Elliott (1781–1849)

Beautiful River! goldenly shining, Where with the cistus woodbines are twining; (Birklands around thee, mountains above thee,) Rivilin wildest! do I not love thee?

Walking the Rivelin: Trail Route

Malin Bridge to Glen Bridge

1. Grogram Wheel
2. Mousehole Forge
3. Walkley Bank Tilt
   (Havelock Dam)
4. Hollins Bridge Mill
5. Spooners Wheel
6. New Dam
7. Roscoe Wheel
8. Holme Head Wheel
9. Little London Wheel
10. Nether Cut Wheel

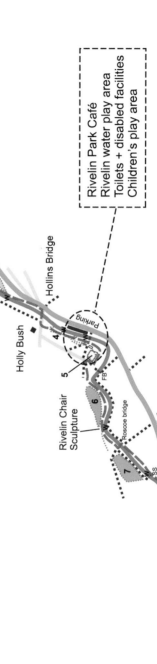

Holme Lane

Supertram terminus

Malin Bridge

River Loxley

START

Loxley Road

River Loxley

Malin Bridge Mill

Rivelin Valley Road

Mousehole/Racker Way bridge

Car park

The Anvil

Stannington Road

FB

SS

1

2

3

Hollins Bridge

Holly Bush

Parking

4

5

Rivelin Chair Sculpture

6

Roscoe bridge

Hagg Hill

7

SS

8

River Rivelin Valley Road

9

10

Glen Bridge ("S Bend")

To Rails Road

Rivelin Park Café
Rivelin water play area
Toilets + disabled facilities
Children's play area